# Quarterly Essay

CONTENTS

| | |
|---|---|
| iii | Foreword *Amanda Lohrey* |
| 1 | **VOTING FOR JESUS** <br> Christianity and Politics in Australia <br> *Amanda Lohrey* |
| 80 | CORRESPONDENCE <br> *Rebecca Huntley, Guy Rundle, Andrew Norton, Ben Oquist, Christopher Theunissen, Don Aitkin, Clive Hamilton* |
| 112 | Contributors |

Quarterly Essay is published four times a year by Black Inc., an imprint of Schwartz Publishing Pty Ltd
Publisher: Morry Schwartz

ISBN 186-395-230-6
ISSN 1832-0953

Subscriptions (4 issues): $49 a year within Australia incl. GST (Institutional subs. $59). Outside Australia $79. Payment may be made by Mastercard, Visa or Bankcard, or by cheque made out to Schwartz Publishing. Payment includes postage and handling.

To subscribe, fill out and post the subscription card, or subscribe online at:

www.quarterlyessay.com

Correspondence and subscriptions should be addressed to the Editor at:

Black Inc.
Level 5, 289 Flinders Lane
Melbourne VIC 3000 Australia
Phone: 61 3 9654 2000
Fax: 61 3 9654 2290
Email:
quarterlyessay@blackincbooks.com (editorial)
subscribe@blackincbooks.com (subscriptions)

Editor: Chris Feik
Management: Sophy Williams
Production Co-ordinator: Caitlin Yates
Publicity: Anna Lensky
Design: Guy Mirabella

# FOREWORD

The fraught relationship between religion and politics has come to the fore in recent times and seems to have crystallised around two moments in 2004, one in July when Federal Treasurer Peter Costello addressed a large congregation of the faithful at Sydney's Hillsong Church in Baulkham Hills – "we need a return to faith and values which made our country strong" – and the other when the new political party Family First, a party based on the Assemblies of God churches of which Hillsong is a prominent member, had its first senator, Steve Fielding, elected to federal parliament. Suddenly the press was full of church and state issues, as if they had not always been with us (though with rather less singing and swaying). Labor's Kevin Rudd pronounced that not since the ALP Split in the '50s had politics and religion come together in such a significant way. The conservative parties had set out to hijack religion for political purposes, he said, and Labor needed to respond.

Costello's rousing appearance wasn't the first time a Liberal politician had graced the Hillsong premises: in October 2002, Prime Minister John Howard had opened its new $25 million convention centre in Baulkham Hills. In July 2005, Costello spoke again to thousands at the Hillsong annual convention at Sydney Olympic Park's SuperDome and proclaimed the gathering a "blessing to the Australian nation". This time, around twenty other Coalition politicians were in the audience, including Alexander Downer, Helen Coonan and Kevin Andrews. Labor's Bob Carr also addressed the convention and described the "spontaneity and informality" of Hillsong's worship as "very Australian". Did this mean that the ritual and formal liturgy of the mainstream churches as practised since white settlement was "un-Australian"? Clearly we had entered into a new arena of public rhetoric; vague, opportunistic, and at times even bizarre.

What has prompted this apparent rush of blood to the head of the Australian body politic, and how seriously should we take it? Are we dealing with anything new, or just an old campaigner dressed up in some bright new Hallelujah clothes? And how real or tendentious is the case, currently being made by spokespersons on the so-called Christian Right, for a groundswell in theologically based moral and political conservatism?

Debates in the area of religion and politics can often be dry and legalistic, as in the matter of High Court cases regarding church and state, or bitter and abrasive, as in the great Split in the ALP in the 1950s and the campaigns of the National Civic Council. Much of what is visible in these wars for what Winston Churchill once described as "empires of the mind" is combative, worldly and faction-ridden. In the public arena the profoundly personal, experiential nature of religious experience becomes occluded, as if this were some mere epiphenomenon of doctrine, rather than its abiding justification and anchorage. When we turn to reports in the media what we find mostly is the clamour of the patriarchs – politicians, pastors and bishops – and less from the congregations of the faithful that they presume to represent. But any accounting of the faithful soon reveals a spectrum of dissidents, or at the very least individuals privately pursuing their spiritual life in a realm of freedom of conscience that, ironically, is guaranteed them not by their religious faith but by the secular state.

It troubles me when I hear the bishops and Christian politicians pontificate. How accurately do they represent the individual's faith and experience? Who is speaking for whom? For this reason I have chosen a somewhat unorthodox form for this essay, in which I book-end it with the voices of ordinary believers, those who are not in the public eye. Pundits who trumpet a Christian revival claim that it is especially marked among the young and so I have chosen young Christians to speak to: those who have yet to make an entry into the fray of public certainty and are still absorbed in finding a way through to a faith that speaks authentically to their own understanding and experience. In these voices we hear the complexity, subtlety and, often, unpredictability of individual moral reasoning; a sphere of freedom, within or without religious discourse, that the secular state exists to preserve and protect.

Amanda Lohrey

# VOTING FOR JESUS

## Christianity and Politics in Australia

Amanda Lohrey

## THE COOL GIRLS

It's a dark wet afternoon beneath one of those Sydney skies of low turbid cloud and I am sitting in the bedroom of a sixteen-year-old schoolgirl whom I'll call Abby. Abby has invited her friends Rebecca and Skye to join us and we are here to talk about the spirit. For some time Abby's parents have been telling me about their daughter's involvement in the Hillsong Church and her regular attendance at one of its youth groups, and Abby and her friends have agreed to be interviewed on the subject of their religious convictions. These girls interest me because none of them has Christian parents. At the tender ages of fifteen and sixteen they have found their own way to faith. They are the new foot soldiers for Jesus.

Abby's room is a conventional teenager's room. There are no altars or crucifixes, or any kind of religious iconography; just a double bed draped with a mosquito net, some silk cushions, posters, a guitar upright in the corner, a desk and computer, ornaments, books and a rogue's gallery of photos on a posterboard on the wall. The usual. Nor could these three girls be described as pious. These are cool girls: good-looking, into pop music, and with a dynamic circle of friends. They are also scholastically bright, as their school results attest. But they strike me as being very different in character, one from another. Abby sits demurely at her desk chair. She is pretty and she is serious; quiet and thoughtful. Skye leans against the old fireplace and seems restless. She says least of the three but soon reveals an insouciant wit with a gleam of take-it-or-leave-it confidence in her eye. But it is Rebecca, sprawled on the bed, who is the forceful centre of the group. A handsome and intelligent girl, she impresses me as articulate and a born organiser; a kind of young Athena of zealous character sprung fully formed from, in this case, the head of Jehovah. It is Rebecca who is the most wary of me. She knows that Hillsong has been in the news recently and suspects that I have come to run some kind of exposé; to set her up.

And maybe I have.

I explain to the Hillsong girls that I'm writing for the *Quarterly Essay* series and they agree to let me tape them. What is immediately interesting is how honest and open they are, and how comfortable they appear in expressing their differences in front of one another. Clearly they have discussed the issues I raise before, among themselves, and are willing to accept that friends may differ. Despite disagreements on, say, abortion, they are comfortable in speaking their mind, and to co-exist, for now, in the same Christian youth group because what matters – fundamentally and above all "issues" – is having a relationship with Jesus. Jesus is the key to all things and the test of every action is "What would Jesus do?"

I ask Abby if she can remember when she first became interested in Jesus. "Well," she begins, "I started going to Youth [Hillsong] about two years ago because some of my friends were going and they said it was fun and that's when I got interested in Jesus. I believed in God before that and I believed in Jesus but I didn't have a relationship with him."

*You feel you now have a relationship with him?*

"Yes, it's like, it's the relationship with Jesus that they offer you, not the religion. It's more like, do you want Jesus to come into your life and to love him?"

This is my first encounter with a distinction that is to come up again and again, the difference between having a personal relationship with Jesus and "religion". It soon becomes clear that in Abby's mind religion is a set of rules and institutional practices that she does not relate to and that can seem arcane, musty and even comical (later in the course of our conversation she will indulge in witheringly satirical mimicry of one of the Christian ministers who recently visited her school).

Jesus, on the other hand, is something else. "Like, ultimately he died for me and I think that's really awesome."

I ask the girls what "God" means to them. *Is Jesus a form of God?*

Abby: "There's a God and Jesus is his son. God sees the earth is dying and he'll give a part of himself in Jesus to save the earth. Jesus is God on earth, God in a form we can cope with."

God in a form we can cope with? This strikes me as quite a sophisticated thought. And I note the use of the present tense, that the earth is perpetually in a state of dying and the gift of Jesus and his redemption of the earth is a perpetual, ongoing process, not a one-off event that occurred two millennia ago.

I turn to Rebecca, who tells me that her older brother has been her primary influence. "He began attending a Baptist church about five years ago and then he heard about Hillsong and started going and he told me about it."

*Why did your brother start going to the Baptist Church?*

"Well, because initially the guy who runs the Baptist Church was teaching scripture at our school and they used to give out free hot chips on a Friday and my brother started going because of that, and that's how he got started."

The girls look at one another and break into laughter.

"Yeah, hot chips," echoes Skye.

"Well, he's a boy," murmurs Abby.

I ask Rebecca if her parents are Christians and she says no. "I think my mum believes in God, she just doesn't really feel the need to have him in her life. My dad is a scientist and he believes in evolution."

*Don't some Christians believe in evolution?*

"Yeah, my mum believes in evolution but she thinks that probably God's behind it, or something."

*What differences did you and your brother find between the Baptist Church you went to and Hillsong?*

"Baptists bring everything back to the Bible. Hillsong brings absolutely everything back to the Bible but I think they put it much more like, you can have it now. Like these old things can still relate to now time. Everything from the Bible they relate back to today."

*Don't the Baptists teach this as well?*

"Yeah, they do, but they don't necessarily relate it so much back to real life."

*It seems a bit more like something in a book?*

"Yeah. I think a lot of Catholic and other Christians are very caught up with the rules of Christianity and stuff, which is what most people see, but it's not really about that. Like Abby said, it's not really about religion, it's about having a relationship with Jesus."

On 13 January 2006, the *Sydney Morning Herald* blogger Andrew West wrote a piece on young evangelical Christians that produced a big rush from young correspondents, many of whom made the same point. "Please do not confuse God with religion," wrote one. "Religion is an instrument of humanity, not of God." This sounds like a restatement of the fundamental principle of the Protestant Reformation, namely that no one or no thing should come between the individual soul and its God.

If only it were that simple.

"But there must be some rules in your group," I say.

"There's not so much rules," Rebecca replies, "there's guidelines, stuff like the Ten Commandments and you shouldn't swear and you shouldn't take drugs, don't have sex before you get married. I think if you look at every single rule in the Bible, they're all there to protect you from things that in the end are going to hurt you. Like even if having sex before marriage mightn't hurt you, you get attached and you're gonna get your heart broken ... But if you break the rules, it doesn't mean that you're not a Christian."

*So if you do break the rules, what's the reaction from the group?*

"Well, you don't get expelled or anything. It's just, like, if you want to tell someone about it they'll just talk to you and there are leaders or older mentors who are there for talking about stuff."

Abby intervenes to tell me about youth "cells". These are teenage support groups that meet weekly at the home of either of the cell's two mentor figures (young women in their early twenties). These meetings are clearly something the girls enjoy and look forward to, although they joke about how they have to stop speaking of "cell" groups because of the association with terrorism.

"Yeah," says Skye, "like we're terrorists for Jesus." They giggle.

I have tried so far to be neutral but at this point cannot resist a skewed question. "Is God masculine?" I ask (this is an all-girl enclave, after all).

Abby tells me about a girl they know called Ella who wrote a paper on that subject for her HSC, a paper in which she argued that God is not gendered. "It was really interesting," says Abby.

*What did it say?*

The girls are vague about the argument (it was some time ago) but indicate they are receptive to the idea.

*So why do we say "he"?*

Abby: "It's just tradition, I suppose. Like if you say 'she' you're kind of making a big thing of it when it's not really that ..." She searches for the word, "... relevant. There's quite a lot of women preachers at Hillsong, which is nice because they can relate to you as a girl. But I don't think about that much, probably because, with the women's rights thing, like, now we've got them all."

I let that pass. They're too young to know, to have tested out, which of the "women's rights" they've really "got" and which are only apparent. Right now I'm more interested in that fraught question of "rules", and with it, sin and damnation. On this matter the girls are concerned to make it clear that there is a degree of tolerance in their youth group. Rebecca and Abby believe strongly in no sex before marriage, but some couples in their group are having sex and they are not "shunned" for it. Abby tells me that at summer camp they were given a sex talk by a woman preacher, who explained how she had had sexual partners before marriage and now regretted it. As the preacher explained it, it's like a process of negative imprinting, where each time you have sex you leave behind a little piece of yourself "like the print coming off a piece of paper until the print is all worn away".

Rebecca chimes in: "It's like, every time you have sex with someone, you give away a little bit of yourself to that person. So you should make sure it's the right person, because if you just throw it away then you're definitely going to regret it." Later in the conversation we loop back to this and the imprinting metaphor appears in another, reverse version. This time it's bits of other people you have sex with that stick to you, and you end up carrying a lot of "baggage". "And you get to be a piece of paper that's like, either hollow or it's got all this baggage, all these bits, colours, stuff sticking to it. There are people our age who are having sex and I guarantee you most of them will regret it – like, how I lost my virginity in an elevator."

Skye grimaces. "Yeah. Charming."

I see in this a kind of strategic sense for young girls, a need to find a safe zone to be in while they wait until they are ready. My generation rebelled against the puritan hypocrisy of its elders and fought for sexual freedom, especially for women, but "freedom" can become as despotic as puritan repression. I think of that old warhorse Norman Mailer, who declared recently that it would be "nice" if we could abolish the '60s sexual revolution, and its excesses, and "go back and start again". I think of the sixteen-year-old I know who lives in an outback town in Queensland who confided in me recently that she was being taunted and mocked in her peer group for still being a virgin. "I just haven't met anyone yet that I want to have sex with," she said, deeply resentful of the pressures towards sexual conformity. And perhaps some girls have a sense of having been devalued by the sexually exploitative images of women that are everywhere in the culture and continue to be demeaning. In a Christian youth group they find a sense of the consecration of their bodies as having singular worth. But this is not the old puritanism and should not be mistaken for it. On the other hand, have any of them yet experienced real sexual awakening? Will they feel the same way when they are twenty-five, or even twenty-one?

So what about these rules? *There's no sex before marriage, and what else?*

Abby: "Everyone has different ideas. Like Skye believes in abortion and Rebecca doesn't. Everyone has their different beliefs."

I'm glad they raised it and not me. *So it's alright to disagree about certain things, like abortion?*

"Yeah."

I ask Skye for her views on this most fraught of subjects for Christians and she is lucid, having clearly had reason to rehearse her argument. "We don't know for certain when the baby's soul enters the mother's body," she shrugs. "There's nothing in the Bible about that. If Jesus appeared to us today and said that it definitely is there from the first moment, then I might be against abortion. But it could be that until the baby is born it's part of the mother so the mother should have the say up until then."

Rebecca: "My brother says it's murder."

Abby: "I think you have to look at the outcome. Like if you ban abortion, the woman might go and get one anyway under unhygienic conditions and die."

*So for you, being in favour of abortion is a lesser of two evils thing?*

Abby: "Well, I'm not in favour of it as a general thing but I think it should stay legal."

So these then are my three types, the hardliner (Rebecca), the free-thinker (Skye) and the moderate (Abby). Does this mean that "sin" for them is a slippery concept? How much leeway do they have with the rules before they are damned in eternal fire and brimstone?

*What does being "saved" mean to you?*

Rebecca is in her element here. Despite Ella's speculative HSC paper she is the group's unhesitating dogmatist. "You get saved basically by just accepting Jesus, by acknowledging that you have sin in your life, you're not perfect and acknowledging that Jesus is the way to make that right, and you say: 'Jesus, I want you into my life.' And once you've got Jesus in your life, basically you're saved."

*What about if you die and you've done some bad things — do you still go to heaven?*

"Yeah, as long as you've accepted Jesus into your life."

Here we have the Protestant doctrine of justification by faith alone, as clearly and unambiguously stated as it could be.

*What about if you're a good person and lead a good life but don't believe in Jesus? Or if you're a Muslim or Hindu and have a love for God and you also think Jesus was a great prophet. You don't think these people could go to heaven?*

Rebecca: "Jesus was above all else. You have to understand that and that's what makes you a Christian."

*So the other people are sincere but basically they're out of luck, because they love God but in the wrong form, or the wrong God.*

"They love God, but they don't understand what Jesus was. They don't understand that he died for our sins so that we didn't have to go to hell. If you just believe that Jesus was a regular prophet, then you can't understand that he died for our sins. But in the end it's really not about what you know and what you don't know, it's do you have a relationship with Jesus. Basically it doesn't matter what you call yourself, or what you've done, if you have a relationship with Jesus, that's it, pretty much."

*And everyone else goes to hell?*

"Yeah, much as it sucks, you have to understand that Jesus was the only saviour."

"Much as it sucks ..." This is a phrase that, in the present context, has a certain charm because Rebecca is deploying it as a form of tact; the rueful colloquialism is a concession to me, to soften the message. She does not want to be rude, to suggest the brutal despatch with which I might one day be consigned to hell. At the same time, her honesty and characteristic forthrightness cannot fudge the essential message.

Abby sees it differently. "I don't think people who aren't Christian are going to go to hell," she says, "and I think it's really immature to mock other religions. Like we had this guy come in to religious education at school once and he was making fun of Buddhists and other people and I think that's immature."

*Do you get into arguments about this?*

"It's hard to bring that up in front of other people because that's what they strongly believe, so I feel it's my personal belief and I don't need to discuss it with anyone. I just keep it to myself, except with Rebecca and stuff ... Some people who come to [Hillsong] Youth haven't thought about things much before, so they tend to take on the whole package without thinking it out for themselves."

It's on the tip of my tongue to ask Abby what she means by "immature", but I decide not to press it. She has been brave in speaking out at youth group and stating her convictions, but she is not of an argumentative caste of mind. And despite her differing with Rebecca on this fundamental point, their friendship remains intimate and unwavering. Such are the mysteries of human relationship, even at this age.

There are many more questions I would like to ask, but time is running out and I opt to make my last question somewhat political: *Are you asked to give money at Youth meetings?*

Abby: "Yeah. I'm not sure I should be commenting on this because it's just my personal opinion but like, with giving money, you don't have to give a big amount. If you give a dollar, it's something that means something to you, to help build up the church."

*Are there any guilt trips laid on you if you don't give?*

"They do bring up the point that you could go and spend that money on McDonalds after, or you could give it to something that's helping young people."

*So there is a bit of a guilt trip?*

"Yeah, but I don't really feel guilty."

This provokes another outburst of laughter from the girls, and at that point Abby's father comes into the room and signals that time is up and he is ready to drive them to a cell meeting. They stand, and Rebecca adjusts her hair in the mirror while Abby leans into my tape recorder and swoons mockingly: "Goodbye. I love you." And the girls laugh and rock out of the room and off to "cell", whose name has been changed but is still used. They are animated and clearly looking forward to it.

Some weeks after I speak to the girls I look in on Philip Almond, professor of Comparative Religion at the University of Queensland. In the course of our conversation he describes "the three arms of religious belief" as reason, the Word and religious feeling. Traditional evangelicalism focuses on the Word (of the Bible), whereas Pentecostalism, which includes the new megachurches like Hillsong, is based on the exaltation of religious feeling over reason. We discuss the ways in which moral reason and feeling relate within the Pentecostal model and I tell him about Abby and her dissent from the view that only Christians go to heaven.

For Abby, it is not reasonable that a loving God would condemn good and virtuous individuals from another tradition of faith to eternal suffering. Nor does it feel right that God would be so harsh. I suggest to Philip that this seems a clear instance of how the individual conscience arrives at a position informed by moral reasoning and accords this reasoning primacy over all other sources of authority, scripture included. Yes, he says, and if the individual is psychologically comfortable with this, it works for them. But not everyone is. Some people, he observes, need more certainty than others.

Rebecca, Abby and Skye represent only a small proportion of people their age. In a poll conducted on behalf of the Christian Research Association, only 15 per cent of young Australians said they were "enthusiastically involved in religion" and only 49 per cent believe in God. In another and larger study of young people in church schools, only 9 per cent said school religious education classes were important, while family and friends ranked at 75 per cent. Many young people were not bothered about whether or not there was a God or by their uncertainty: "friendship and family life gave them a sense of purpose in the world." But for those young people who are committed, how likely is it that their faith will endure?

Religious convictions in the young, like radical politics, have a way of settling down into something worn lightly on the sleeve in later life. Sometimes they dissolve altogether into indifference, or even strong antagonism. Will Rebecca, Abby and Skye still be as fervent, and as certain, when they're thirty?

In asking this question my mind turns to the experience of the philosopher and academic Phil Dowe. When I was living in Hobart in the late '90s, I heard a great deal about Dowe, then aged thirty-nine, as a charismatic lecturer in philosophy at the University of Tasmania. He was also an evangelical Christian who ran extra-curricular SUS groups – Scriptures Under Scrutiny – that were popular with students. Knowing this, I was very surprised one morning to open the local paper and find an account of how Dowe had experienced a personal crisis in his faith that had culminated in his leaving the church.

Now, some years later, I find myself teaching on the same campus as Dowe and I seek him out. Dowe grew up in country New South Wales with a father who was an Anglican priest with low-church fundamentalist views. As a "churched-out" schoolboy he turned away from Christianity but returned as a university student. When in 1995 he took up an appointment in the philosophy department at the University of Tasmania, he began attending St John's Presbyterian Church, run by the charismatic preacher David Jones, a fundamentalist. I remembered Jones from the aftermath of the Port Arthur massacre, when he was critical of the inclusion of short prayers from other religions into the memorial service in St David's Anglican Cathedral. Like many others, I was pleasantly surprised, and consoled, by this ecumenical inclusion. It seemed to symbolise the unity of a community that, in the face of pointless and horrific death, had more in common than not. But for Jones the essential point was that the inclusion of these non-Christian prayers meant that the memorial service could not, ipso facto, be a Christian service and therefore could not be consoling to genuine Christians.

Dowe's SUS courses – lunch-time Bible lectures and five-week evening programs – aimed to present the Christian message in a way that was intellectually challenging. It was, he says, a Bible study group for students that was about developing your brain at the level of your studies rather than "leaving the religious part of your brain behind at the Sunday school level". Students didn't have to be Christians to attend, but there was an emphasis on producing converts.

So how did Dowe move from becoming a key figure in the evangelical youth movement to a momentous and painful upheaval in his personal life such that he describes himself today as an "informed agnostic"? There were two principal factors, he tells me. The first was that he became troubled by the politics of fundamentalism and its exclusionary tendency. When I ask him to elaborate on this, he simply nominates a number of issues: gays, women, euthanasia, abortion. He was, he points out, never a creationist, and reminds me that not all evangelicals are, in that sense, fundamentalists. "My own modus operandi in the world has never changed," he says, meaning he has always been an intellectual and at a certain point he could make no moral sense of, for example, a punitive view of homosexuality. When he looked to church leaders for a defence of this stricture – among others – he was disappointed at the calibre of the arguments he encountered.

But even more to the point was a strikingly practical – one might even say scientific – test that this philosopher applied to himself and those around him. The acid test of fundamentalist Christian faith was this: did it make you a better person? Dowe asked this of himself and others, including church leaders, and came up with a negative. "There is a hardcore belief in justification by faith alone as essential to being a Christian. There's a whole theory of the individual being inhabited by the Spirit and how it's supposed to make you a better person. But," he says, in his quiet emphatic way, "it doesn't. Teachings were being applied but they weren't working, they weren't making a difference." Later he remarks that "psychological damage is done in any group with strong leaders" but is not inclined to elaborate, other than to say that what he saw as a leading evangelical, up close and personal, was a god not of compassion but of demonising and scapegoating. When I ask him why such a figure might appeal to young people, he observes that many young Christians are *reactionary* conservatives, that is, they are reacting to cultural change. They look around them and see few places to find a safe mooring. The Bible seems to offer clear and definitive answers. This then makes them vulnerable to fundamentalist edicts on sex, which he describes tersely as "a way of controlling young people".

Phil Dowe's story is not so unusual. I remember as an adolescent attending a public lecture given by Douglas Hyde, a renegade from the British Communist Party and newly converted Catholic. In the fervid atmosphere of packed town halls across the country – this was the height of the Cold War – this Hyde Park–trained orator told the dramatic story of how he had seen the light, how the beauty of the gothic cathedrals had saved him from the dreary, stripped-back utilitarianism of the Marxist credo. (Ever the skeptic, even at the age of fourteen, it seemed to me that Hyde's great love of mediaeval art and music had been a significant influence on his conversion, which might well have been the outcome of a bad dose of aesthetic and sensory deprivation.) Apostates are nothing new and come in all shapes and sizes. What strikes me about Phil Dowe's experience, putting aside the personal and psychological factors that might have influenced him, is the "test" that he came to articulate on the basis of moral reasoning: does religion make you a better person, a better parent, a better neighbour and, above all, in the context of this essay and its concerns, a better citizen?

For the cool girls from Hillsong, politics is not yet an issue. For now, the slings and arrows of citizenship debates fire above their heads. They are uninterested in elections and concerned only to find a meaningful explanation for their lives and a moral compass to guide them through the hormonal wars of adolescence. They can even be scornful of the affluence that has educated them. Abby's mother tells me that Skye once complained to her that her parents thought only about money. "They go to investment seminars," she added with a scornful expression. This is the idealism of youth that has not yet had to pay bills, but it makes me wonder at how they will react to the larger issues in their own church when they are older, a church that preaches the so-called Prosperity Gospel and funds its expansion on the big sell.

# SELLING THE SACRED

The night after I talk to the cool girls I sit up late watching some DVDs sold by the Hillsong Church. First up is a service conducted by Pastor Brian Houston out at the splendid new centre at Baulkham Hills, a big bright auditorium that resembles a concert arena, with a wide stage and cinema-sized screen featuring slickly produced commercials for Hillsong products. Outside there are security guards and Gloria Jeans coffee carts (the Gloria Jeans franchise for Australia is owned by Hillsong elder Nabi Saleh and fellow Hillsong member Peter Irvine).

Pastor Brian Houston is by now a familiar media image. A slim, middle-aged man in glasses and a snappy suit, he paces the stage in a style that is friendly and engaging, if somewhat manic. There is none of the tremulous incantation or portentous gloom of the old fire-and-brimstone preachers, more a kind of gee-up rhetoric familiar to anyone who has ever sat through a coach's half-time address. It's a free-wheeling rave on salvation that doesn't stand much analysis, either for or against; lively but largely inchoate. Houston strikes me as a good working preacher, but no Billy Graham. The comparison is probably unfair, but I heard Billy Graham preach when I was young and he made a great impression on me, so it's inevitable that he should come to mind now. Graham was one of the great orators of the twentieth century, with an almost uncanny stillness and poise. His very demeanour – forget the message – could suggest that he was channelling the Source. This, combined with his good looks, made him perversely seductive in his appeal. But, above all, he had gravitas, the very quality that suggested a stern and magnificent Jehovah might indeed be a reality somewhere out there in the realms of space. Houston, by contrast, resembles a motivational speaker, the very picture of dynamic movement, and indeed on the DVD I'm watching he seems to suggest that salvation is all about moving forward. There is insistent repetition of the words *growth, increase, change, momentum*, all words used by business, and in its own way this is a kind of corporate religious-speak, punctuated by its own commercials for the sale of a CD of the speech currently being delivered, and concluding with the injunction of a good CEO to his shareholders: "Remember, the best is yet to come."

It's more apt to compare Houston with one of his US contemporaries and counterparts, Franklin Graham (son of Billy), who is in the portentous American mould, though without his father's charm and gravitas. Graham Jnr is often stern, and abrasive in his condemnation of other religions, such as Islam, while in his sermons he tends to talk a lot about "sin" and "the sinner". He is in the traditional mould of the messianic orator and shares in the general American sense of apocalyptic exceptionalism: "We're living in the last days." Houston – originally from New Zealand – is more of a Downunder model, with a kind of eager, neighbourly cheerfulness that is mostly about feeling good and accentuating the positive. He seems to suggest that if you are constantly feeling bad about yourself then you are not much use either to you or anyone else, and there is something of modern psychology in this. He defends his Prosperity Gospel on the grounds that the more money you have, the more you can give away to help others. Put like this it sounds eminently reasonable, although many other evangelicals, on both the liberal and fundamentalist wings, are disapproving of his message as altogether too redolent of New Ageism.

This is an aspect of Hillsong that has been widely deplored: its easy adoption of the commercial culture of the mass media. Its defenders argue that this is merely a matter of style and that there is no point in objecting to it as morally deficient unless you want to repudiate the whole of postmodern culture and its forms of communication. If you see religion as a counter to this, you risk being categorised by the young as reactionary, fuddy-duddy and fit for the retirement home. This was brought home to me when I listened to some young people discussing their recent attendance at a Franklin Graham crusade in Melbourne in 2005. One complained of Graham being "a bit old" and that his talk was not "pitched enough to youth". Another complained that the music was "too subdued", unlike the Pentecostal church she attended where it was more "flamboyant and out there".

The fact that Houston and Hillsong have come to greater public prominence than other evangelical preachers and congregations seems to be a matter of good management with regard to style and presentation, rather than any distinctive message. Hillsong is a razzle-dazzle outfit and people quite simply have a good time there. Another evangelical outfit not all that far away in the same city, the Christian City Church, has a similar infrastructure of groups, training courses and conferences (the "Real Men" ministry and conferences and their "Everywoman" version, as well as business courses that teach the Prosperity Gospel). Its leaders, husband-and-wife team Phil and Chris Pringle, are even Brian and Bobbie Houston look-alikes. So why are their congregations smaller and why don't we hear about them in the media?

In part because they are not yet a "megachurch". A megachurch is usually defined as one that has an average congregation of more than 2,000 per weekend – churches like Hillsong and the Paradise Church in South Australia claim weekend attendances of up to 20,000. In the US in 1960 there were fewer than ten of these and now there are over 1,200, with three currently able to boast of weekend figures of 20,000-plus. How did this come about?

Robert Putnam, the author of Bowling Alone, an acclaimed study of the decline of civic organisations in America over the last forty years, argues for the success of the megachurches as a new form of community for the lonely and the dislocated. Traditionally churches of all denominations fulfilled an important function as civic clubs, but cultural transformation left many of them seeming musty and outmoded. In recognition of this, the pastors of two of North America's biggest megachurches, Willow Creek Church in Chicago and Saddleback in California, conducted a survey of those in their area who did not go to church and asked them what they disliked about it and what would persuade them to come along. In response to this consumer research the pastors completely redesigned their churches along the lines of the shopping mall and entertainment centre. "Out went 200-year-old hymns, pulpits and even church-like buildings. In came information booths, food courts, churches that look like schools, reggae services and sermons with PowerPoint presentations."

The traditional church relied on organic community and continuity among the generations of one family, but increased geographical mobility means that many people are now less likely to live in the community they grew up in. When they move, they seek new and instant sources of community and a network of contacts they can plug into. It's easy to connect up with a church like Saddleback that has 2,600 small groups – "for computer nerds, cyclists, knitters, you name it" – co-ordinated by a large ministry. (This is reflected in Hillsong, not least in the network of youth cells that Rebecca, Abby and Skye so enjoy participating in, even if, as they confessed to me, they rarely discuss religion there.) "The megachurches", writes Putnam, "are providing community bonds on the new frontier of America's middle-class migrants," and this too applies in Australia, where a megachurch service will always feature a number of recent immigrants and Asian students. At the Franklin Graham rally, for instance, a Hong Kong student talked about the importance of "belonging".

Houston, with the aid of singer-songwriter Darlene Zschech, has refashioned Christian worship as a party-cum-pop-concert. The importance of upbeat contemporary music to Hillsong's success is reflected in the fact that the church was originally named Hills Christian Life Centre, but acquired its current name organically because the music was such a feature that it quickly came to define the character of the worship. Every service features live singers and bands of professional calibre and a form of Christian rock music so appealing, even to some non-Christians, that Hillsong's many CDs generate substantial income. For years, churches have tried to incorporate contemporary music into their services but too often the results were daggy and amateurish, a cross between bad garage band and pub singalong (not unlike the dreary improvised folksongs sometimes heard at environment rallies or anti-logging sites). It's amazing what a professional sound will do and several Hillsong albums, recorded live at church gatherings, have debuted in the top four of the ARIA charts. It is clear even from watching the televised services – and this is borne out in accounts of people who attend live services – that being at Hillsong is like being at a big rock festival.

I've written elsewhere on the power of music in general, and singing in particular, to affect human physiology and release endorphins – to create a natural high – so it comes as no surprise to me to observe the degree to which participation in quality "now" music is at the centre of the Hillsong experience, and not just for the young. It's easy to forget that part of the appeal of early Methodism in England was the singing of rousing new hymns in colloquial English, a music that Charles Wesley's "ordinary working folk" could relate to. It was also the case that in writing his 9,000 or so hymns Wesley drew on what we would now describe as popular culture.

It is no coincidence that the first winner of *Australian Idol* came directly out of the major Pentecostal centre in Adelaide, the Paradise Church, one that's affiliated with the Assemblies of God churches in Australia (AOG), the organisation of which Brian Houston is president. Philip Almond describes a megachurch service as "a perfect mesh" of religion and popular culture, one that "mimics religion as event in the way that a mediaeval cathedral used to, full of smoke, sound, colour and music". On feast-days especially, the cathedrals would be surrounded by colourful booths, jugglers, fire-eaters and bands of drummers performing the Passion Plays. Hillsong and Paradise are large enough to provide an all-encompassing experience in the way that your average parish can't (even if its members had the inclination). And this, according to Almond, leads to a second smoke-and-mirrors factor, namely that the megachurches are not growing at the dramatic rate their depiction in the media would suggest. "What attracts the media", he says, "is a showbiz quality that mirrors the flashy celebrity obsession of the media itself. But are the mass audiences – up to 20,000-plus at weekends – indicative of real growth overall?" Almond seeks to administer a reality check, drawing attention to the fact that new Pentecostal churches are not springing up in every suburb. "People are travelling to the megachurches because of their high profile and they get this much higher profile, more than they deserve, than if the same number of people were dispersed throughout the parishes as the Anglicans are, or the Catholics." In other words, don't count your Christians in one spot (megachurch), count them across the board.

But Christians in one spot are convenient; a more convenient mass assembly for politicians to address and attempt to mobilise. Just as industrialisation and the rise of mass employment in factories made it easier to unionise workers, the megachurches make it easier, if not to mobilise a growing political influence, then to create the illusion of one, which, in modern media terms, amounts to much the same thing. Spectacle televises well. A massed crowd is a powerful image; it sends a message in itself. As the American writer Don DeLillo wrote in his 1991 novel *Mao II*, "The future belongs to crowds." And who cares if those same people are still there two years on? According to Cheryl Catford, Principal of Tabor College, a Pentecostal-based theological college in Melbourne, Pentecostalism has one of the highest drop-out rates of any religious denomination, and few of those who drop out go on to other churches. How much conversion, she asks, converts into "discipleship"? How much in the way of smoke and mirrors are we dealing with here? The answer is important, not least because in future the Pentecostal "phenomenon", an alleged groundswell, is going to be used by right-wing politicians to belabour the rest of us.

Gary Bryson of the ABC's *Encounter* religion program argues that there is nothing new in the showbiz phenomenon that is Hillsong – that throughout its history Pentecostalism has sought to replicate the host culture by using its forms of communication. The evangelicals used mass meetings and cheap printing; the Pentecostals quickly discovered first radio and then television. The fact that churches are now more consumerised simply reflects changes in the host culture. In 2004, Hillsong, on Brian Houston's estimate, had an income of 50 million dollars, tax-free. A significant proportion of that came from donations and the sale of "product". Here is how the young writer Alice Bell saw it when she attended the 2005 Hillsong Conference at the Homebush Olympic Stadium:

> At one point the lights go down. People scream like they did at the Alice Cooper concert. They all pull out their mobile phones, using them as electronic candles and waving them in the dark. It looks incredible. Then come the songs again: "I will love you forever", "How Great is Our God" and my personal favourite, "Holy, Holy, I am here". We sing and sing and sing ... Church owner Brian Houston jumps onto stage like an excited puppy and grabs the microphone. "*That was so good! That was so good I think God wants to hear it again! One more Holy Holy!*" ... We finish for a second time, waiting for Brian's praise. We have worked hard. Surely we are worthy. He recovers his breath and we all lean forward, eager for his words of wisdom ... instead we are met with ... "*Ahhh ... the DVD. I pray you buy this for your family. I pray that you buy this for your friends. Amen.*" My mouth drops. He just "amen-ed" a DVD sale! This is a glorified infomercial! Brian apologises for going on about the DVD packs (I assume this isn't the first time) but he's just "*excited because it's so great!*" The crowd claps again. DVD! CD! Featured extras! Yay!

Not long after, buckets are passed around and Alice is surprised to find that the buckets have a hole in them so that change will drop right through to the floor. It's notes, credit cards or cheque. "*Amen?*" she asks, "or *Amex?*"

Here is religion geared to a generation raised on television and the rapid-fire commercial break. Dr Carole Cusack, a lecturer in religion at the University of Sydney, describes Hillsong's style of worship as more attuned to secular values in the community than that of other denominations. It's not new religion, she argues, but "part of the re-branding of Christianity as fashionable, trendy, not dowdy". In the Pentecostal churches there is and always has been plenty of dancing – or at least plenty of clapping and swaying and waving of arms – but now it has a new, slick look to it. Whereas Pentecostalism was once associated with meetings in private houses or run-down wooden halls in unfashionable suburbs – and this is still the case for some branches – Hillsong is something else. Indeed, in a revealing interview with ABC TV's *Australian Story*, Pastor Brian Houston told of how one of his initial inspirations was a set of television commercials featuring a man who had developed the biggest Holden dealership in Australia: "I thought to myself, if you can build a Holden dealer like that, the largest Holden dealership in Australia, surely it [Baulkham Hills] must be somewhere where you could build a church." Earlier in the same interview he talked about "controlling the franchise" of Hillsong and the Hillsong "brand".

In their utilisation of secular methods, Australian Pentecostals, it seems, even have something to teach their American friends. After a visit to Australia during which he noticed the use of the term "festival" rather than "crusade", Franklin Graham changed the name of his US gatherings. "Crusade is a church term," he announced. "It's a church meeting. You have beer festivals, music festivals, flower festivals, art festivals. It's a secular term. The world understands that term, and it's the world that I'm trying to reach. That's why I made the change. The Australians used the word festival first."

The new megachurches may, as their critics claim, be "theologically shallow", a triumph of contemporary style over substance, but they sure are upbeat. Take the Hillsong Colour Your World women's conference, an event attended by 11,000 women, from several Christian denominations, in Sydney in 2005. This featured a number of women preachers, including Pastor Bobbie Houston, the wife of Hillsong's leader, Pastor Brian. Every one of these preachers fitted a glamorous type that might have been plucked from a wholesome US sitcom. They were slim, with expensive teeth, long (mostly blonde) hair, stiletto heels and dangly earrings. They incarnate an ideal of the consumerised goddess, a set of Barbie look-alikes who refer to themselves as "chicks"; a slightly older version of the women who sell perfume and cosmetics in glamorous television advertisements. At the conference, there were very few trappings of "religion". "We are just girlfriends in the living-room," preached Bobbie Houston, and watching the DVD I was irresistibly reminded of a Tupperware or negligee party. Most of the preaching, it has to be said, is on the level of the banal pep-talk, with the occasional psalm lost in the torrent of feel-good invocations. "Women are fantastic. Turn to the person on one side and say: you are fantastic. You will not die for lack of encouragement in this place." Overall it seems akin to New Age feelgoodism, with Jesus thrown in as a bonus.

How did the 11,000 women present get there? Well, there was the media coverage, and then there was word of mouth. Most of those who attended were already Christians. I interviewed one woman who heard about it at her local hair salon. A strong Lutheran, she went along out of curiosity but decided it wasn't her thing. "Too much singing and not enough thinking," she pronounced, echoing the criticism of Hillsong made by many traditional Christians. There was something else she didn't like about the Colour Your World conference and struggled to articulate, but which could be summed up in the phrase "too globalised". The style of the megachurches, such as Hillsong, is a glitzy, corporatised version of the old revivalist tent, cut loose from any organic community roots, and traditional Christians prefer a church that is more enmeshed, over time, in their local community. They find they are more comfortable in their mini-church, even if they tend to shop around to find an individual pastor who suits their own brand of faith: liberal, moderate or fundamentalist.

Other Christians, including other evangelicals who are critical of the showbiz model of Pentecostalism, tend to fall into two camps: those who suspect it of being too right-wing and those for whom it is not conservative enough. For American nature writer and liberal Methodist Bill McKibben, the North American megachurches represent a degraded theology. They are "a perfect mirror", he writes, of the secular bestseller lists, indeed of the secular culture, with its American fixation on self-improvement, on self-esteem. On self. These similarities make it difficult (although not impossible) for the televangelists to posit themselves as embattled figures in a "culture war" – they offer too uncanny a reflection of the dominant culture, a culture of unrelenting self-obsession.

As I watched the DVDs of the Colour Your World conference, I found myself thinking like an anthropologist, less interested in questions like: is the message true or false, than: is this a new form of cultural home? A kind of community centre, church, gymnasium and entertainment centre rolled into one? Not only is the music good and the services a lot of fun, but there is also a centralised infrastructure of support that addresses many of the concerns of contemporary suburban life, from how to be "masculine" in the postmodern world to how to achieve better health and fitness (one US church boasts the slogan: "Slim for Him").

If you consult the advertising brochures for Hillsong, you will find a range of options on offer. There is a brochure promoting the Hillsong Men's Conference 2006, Dare to Be, which features the back view of a young man in jeans and a white t-shirt, arms outstretched, peroxided hair standing up in gelled spikes, superimposed over an image of a rock band on stage. For something more ongoing you can attend the regular courses on offer. There is the Hillsong LIFE, body+soul+spirit brochure, in which all the models in the photos look as if they have been lifted straight out of *Neighbours* or *Home and Away*.

Courses run as follows:

1. *Body+Soul*
"Back In Shape After Baby"
"Healthy Living" ("Fat Burning" etc.)
2. *Identity and Purpose*
"Search for Life" ("The Origin of Self-doubt, Renewing our Mind Planner" etc.)

"Wild at Heart" ("The Question that Haunts Every Man, The Battle for a Man's Heart")

Among others on offer are "Valiant Man", about "male sexual discipleship"; "Kissed the Girls and Made Them Cry" ("Purity's promise"); "Taming the Tiger" (on anger management); "Mirror, Mirror" (on self-esteem and getting free of abusive relationships).

Because of the glossy and upbeat image you can go along to any of these courses without feeling a "loser" and this, it turns out, is important. In a recent survey conducted on behalf of the Bible Society of NSW, market researchers found that many people see having anything to do with church as an admission of personal failure. "The problem we detected from our research was that a lot of Australians see Christianity as being for losers," says Angus Kinnaird, Melbourne strategy director for FutureBrand, a company hired to produce a new advertising campaign for a multi-denominational group of Australian churches. Interestingly, the Paradise and Hillsong churches were not among the churches that commissioned the survey: they figure they've solved the "loser" problem already.

The megachurches offer a whole infrastructure of potential support as long as you can afford it and are willing to pay your "Biblical tithe". On Andrew West's *Sydney Morning Herald* blogsite, one respondent expressed skepticism at the degree to which this support might compare with, say, what is on offer at the Salvation Army, and cited a friend in depressed economic circumstances who went to Hillsong and felt unwelcome. At the Salvos, the writer claimed, she found emotional support and got her electricity bill paid. But the Salvos are often dealing with the desperate – "losers" – and their emergency needs for food and shelter, while the focus of the megachurches is unapologetically middle class, as expressed in the Prosperity Gospel, a Calvinist-derived doctrine in which one of the visible outward signs of God's favour is the affluence of the faithful. When this is brought up, Brian Houston argues that the affluent too have personal problems and "outreach" is not just about working with the poor; he also cites Hillsong's charity projects – $500,000 in tsunami contributions and the church's adoption of an entire district in Uganda.

There is nothing to say that a church has to spend money on charity, but the question becomes a matter of public interest when the organisation has, firstly, been granted a tax-free status and, secondly, received government grants for alleged charity projects. In a 2005 article in *Business Review Weekly*, Adele Ferguson gave a detailed account of just how lucrative a tax-exempt business Hillsong and the Pentecostal churches are: "Pentecostal churches are not waiting to inherit the earth. They are taking it now tax-free." Ferguson detailed some of the business directories, networking groups, conferences and prosperity seminars run by the churches, fuelled by their

> big advantage over the commercial world in that they do not have to pay tax, they do not file tax returns, they get government concessions and grants, much of their workforce is voluntary so they have relatively small wage bills, and there is little accountability and transparency about what they do or how they spend the money.

Ferguson also cited a former general-secretary of the Assemblies of God and Pentecostal preacher, Philip Powell, who describes the new Pentecostal pastors as having "hijacked the godly movement". Many of these ministers "are no more than business magnates who benefit from the tax-free status of corporations that they lead" and who have "cashed in on a loophole in the western governmental tax system". In a recent speech Greens Senator Christine Milne claimed it was unfair to genuine church welfare agencies like Anglicare and St Vincent de Paul when organisations like Hillsong called into question the legitimacy of the current tax-exempt system. "Why start up a business," she asked, "when you can do better by starting a new church?"

A number of questions about federal grants to Hillsong have been asked in federal parliament by Carmen Lawrence, and in December 2005 the

NSW state Labor MP Ian West raised questions about Hillsong's misuse of large federal grants amounting to $414,479 to assist Aboriginal communities. Not long after, Tony Williams, business development manager for the NSW Department of State and Regional Development, made related allegations. The *Australian* newspaper took up the issue, but when approached, Leigh Coleman, spokesperson for Hillsong's benevolent arm, Hillsong Emerge, refused to answer any questions. The *Australian* persisted with its inquiries and ran a report on 13 February 2006 revealing that almost all the money from an indigenous development grant of $315,000 given to Hillsong Emerge had gone to employing and providing offices for church staff. "Hillsong also failed to enable a single Aborigine to become self-employed under a $610,968 federal grant to encourage indigenous entrepreneurship." The report noted that this information was elicited in parliament by Labor's indigenous affairs spokesman, Chris Evans, and that "Labor figures have expressed suspicion about the grants and the Liberal Party's links with Hillsong." The following day's edition of the *Australian* then carried a report that the federal Justice Minister, Chris Ellison, had moved to strip Hillsong of one of its grants ($414,479): the government had clearly gone into damage-control mode. Hillsong Emerge again refused to respond to media requests for a statement and at the time of writing their "charity" projects remain under a cloud.

Other Christians, including other evangelicals, may disapprove of Hillsong's consumerist model, but some of them would like a slice of the action. They are worried about their low rate of church attendance as a percentage of the Australian population and are prepared to embark on some marketing of their own. On 20 September 2005, in an article entitled "The atheist who's selling Jesus", the *Age* reported on Angus Kinnaird and FutureBrand's new marketing strategy for the Christian faith. Market research done by the Bible Society had found a marked resistance to the message. Despite all the ballyhoo in the media about a Christian revival, as regular church-goers Australians still rate at only 9 per cent. Catholic church attendance in Australia declined by an estimated 13 per cent between 1996 and 2001, and Anglican attendance by 2 per cent.

The marketing guru himself is yet to be convinced that his campaign to market Jesus – which has already commenced in parts of Australia – will be a success. Kinnaird, who has advised on the Sydney Olympics and for Telstra, among others, opines: "I've had lots of clients wanting to update their image but I don't think I've ever come across one that has quite as many problems as the church." After two years' research and planning, he decided that the new marketing strategy will "keep the church, the Bible and religion well out of the picture. Instead, the spotlight falls on just one star. Jesus is played not as the son of God but a tough-talking no-nonsense philosopher who makes life easier and, incidentally, eternal."

The outcome is the "Jesus. All About life" campaign, "the most intense and broad-based religious campaign in this country to try to reclaim lost ground". The campaign began in Adelaide in August 2005 with a number of television commercials and radio spots, billboard advertisements and a mail-out of 250,000 postcards. There is also a website and a 126-page booklet that features a "desanitised" saviour, a "gutsy speaker who pulled no punches". In response to the question of "Why Jesus?" Kinnaird says: "That was the only place we had to go. The research shows that the church is an almost insurmountable obstacle to the campaign. The church was seen as the problem, not the solution."

"The classic line is that the church is hopeless but Jesus is cool," says Martin Johnson, communications manager of the NSW Bible Society. The first plan was the punchy slogan: "Jesus. Nothing about Religion". "It was very powerful," Kinnaird says. "It slapped you in the face. But it just wasn't palatable to the churches involved." So the message was softened. In one of the TV ads a young mother says: "You can take or leave religion, but can't get away from the fact that a lot of what Jesus says makes sense."

This theme announced itself at the very beginning of this essay in the answer given to the first question I asked of the Hillsong girls, Abby,

Rebecca and Skye: it's nothing to do with "religion" and it's all about Jesus; "God in a form we can cope with". Jesus has a high recognition factor. Jesus is not a loser. Jesus is young and engaging and known for his personal integrity.

In short, Jesus is a marketing man's dream.

# IMAGO DEI

Christianity is a religion of incarnation, of God become man, and this has given rise to one of the most powerful imaginings, or god-images, produced by any culture. "The soul never thinks without an image," wrote Aristotle, and the divine figures of classical Greek sculpture are a lasting testimony to the beauty of that "thinking". In her classic study of Hindu iconography, the art historian Diana Eck offers a fascinating survey of the evolution of this idea in Western religions, from the Hebraic antagonism to any imagining of the divine to the bleeding hearts of the Pellegrini statues that adorn Catholic bookshops. "On the whole," writes Eck, "it would be fair to say that the Western traditions, especially the religious traditions of the 'Book' – Judaism, Christianity, and Islam – have trusted the Word more than the Image as a mediator of divine truth ... The ears are somehow more trustworthy than the eyes." In the Christian tradition this suspicion of the eyes has been a particularly Protestant position and the brutality of that repudiation of the image can make the visitor gasp, as in the chapel of Ely Cathedral in England where the faces of dozens of statues remain obliterated, smashed by zealots of the Cromwellian era. Nevertheless, if the tendency of the Protestant churches has been to repudiate the visual image as such – other than a bare sign of the cross – the worship of Protestant individuals is powerfully connected to the image of Jesus.

Theologians speak of the *imago dei*, or image of God, and it is clear from even a glancing acquaintance with anthropology that this *imago* takes various forms in different cultures: Jesus may or may not be the one true God, but he is not the only *imago dei* that the human imagination has given birth to. The Hindu pantheon alone has over 3,000 different god-images.

In Christian cultures there is a gap between God as a form or force beyond human understanding and God as an accessible totem, and this is a gap that the Jesus figure has the potential richly to fill. He is, to quote the sixteen-year-old Abby, "God in a form we can cope with" or, as Episcopalian bishop John Shelby Spong writes, Jesus is the gate through which Christians can reach God: "if we didn't have a Jesus figure we would have to invent one." For Christians he is the soul's image of the divine as a figure who can reconcile the dualism of God/man; who can function both as a transcendentally powerfully protector and redeemer and as an infallibly wise and supportive mentor. Even where God the creative principle is given a human form, he may be remote and authoritarian – an elderly patriarch, say, with a white beard, sitting in the clouds. Jesus, on the other hand, is your best friend writ large. To quote Abby again: "The fact that he was prepared to die for me – I find that really awesome."

The historical figure of Jesus has become an intense focus for scholarship, much of it highly contested, including among factions within the Christian churches. Each year hundreds of books are published in several languages, dealing either with the life of Jesus or sources for the authority of his teachings. About the historical Jesus we know almost nothing for certain, other than that he was a young Jew who managed to aggravate the Romans sufficiently for them to crucify him. After that it becomes a welter of competing authorities and radically opposed readings of scripture, from liberal Episcopalians like Spong, who does not believe in a literal Resurrection, to fundamentalists who preach the Second Coming in a not very distant apocalypse in which the bodies of the righteous will be exhumed in good health and carried into a literal Heaven.

Once God becomes man and descends into the grubby world of the material, it is inevitable that this incarnated version of the *imago dei* has the potential to become soiled by association with worldliness. Thus the essential thing for many Christians is that this *imago* is conceived of as free-floating, in the sense of being cut loose from fallible human institutions; that it has a life of its own. Hence the recurring tendency for Jesus' admirers to want to liberate him from his church. No less an institutional figure than Sydney's Anglican Archbishop, Peter Jensen, can say in his 2005 ABC Boyer Lectures, *The Future of Jesus*: "I don't want to talk about the institutional church or even religion. Such things are of marginal interest to me. Even though I quite like going to church, I find it hard to like the institutional organisation. And I don't really think of myself as a religious person." However flagrantly disingenuous it may strike the unsympathetic reader, the statement is intended to connect with an *imago dei* untainted by the failings of human nature, by sectarian disputes and the internal politics of the church as flawed institution. Yet, as theologian Andrew McGowan, Anglican priest and director of the Theological School at Trinity College, Melbourne, has remarked, while there is something "very twenty-first century about a Jesus who isn't religious", the idea of Christianity without religion is not new. "And that religionless Jesus himself, supposedly above history and culture, always becomes the mirror image of the era's own cultural values. 'What would Jesus do?' ends up as something like a nice and thoughtful version of 'What my friends and I would probably like to do anyway'."

A free-floating Jesus suits a corporatised model of religion, such as that of the current megachurches, because it mobilises an already established and powerful god-image in a way that is not hidebound by clericalism and a history of church politics. Cut loose from traditional forms of human authority – the scriptures are not human but the word of God – Jesus can be anything you want him to be; can seem fresh and new while retaining the virtues of the tried and true. In some ways, and I mean no disrespect here, it reminds me of the way in which corporations hire major celebrities to front their image or brand-name. That the brand "Jesus" has massive potential in any era to counter the worldly failings of institutions and their fallible priestly castes is disputed by very few. This is what the NSW Bible Society aims to stress in its advertising campaign. Here is a man, it says, who was an outsider, who stood up to authority, who was true to himself. "Jesus was a square peg in a society of round holes." Since many of us harbour an idea of ourselves as authentic inner rebels while outwardly living a life of modest conformity, this Jesus is an ideal-type pitched to certain aspects of the individual's secret self.

Cultural icons, like U2's Bono, who can't be bothered with "church" or "religion" declare themselves followers of Jesus, but such loose, even hip allegiances are of concern to the Catholic Church's Cardinal George Pell, who says he is worried that Jesus is portrayed as undemanding. Some clergy, like Michael Jensen, lecturer at Sydney University's Moore College, concur. "I feel we have tended to over-emphasise the 'outsider' part of the Jesus story ... he becomes a battler alongside the rest of us battlers." If we are guilty of this "over-emphasis", it may be that this is because "Jesus" is a screen on which we project our own concerns.

Jesus the *imago*, as opposed to the historical figure, is a constant work-in-progress. When I was a student at a Catholic school, the local archbishop came up with the idea of constructing a "teenage Jesus" out of the scriptures, because he thought we might more readily relate to such a figure than to the mature man on the Cross. Special sermons were written and biographical notes given out that emphasised the few episodes in the Bible that dealt with Jesus as a youth. In the end, the archbishop patronised us without success. We found the constructed teenage Jesus uninteresting, indeed vapid, compared to the drama of the crucified Christ. The teenage version died a natural death and was soon no longer heard of – at least not until his resurrection on the cover of Archbishop Jensen's Boyer Lectures, which has Jesus in silhouette with earplugs in his ears and MP3 player in his hand (Dr Jensen, of course, is not responsible for the cover).

There have been many other, and more radical, instances of Jesus revised. There is the well-known case of Thomas Jefferson and the way in which that devout Christian and slave-owner sat up for many evenings cutting bits out of the Bible that he didn't like – and what he mostly didn't like were the miracles, or anything that smacked of the supernatural (like walking on water). As a man of action and a man of Reason – a Christian of the Enlightenment – he took scissors and paste and excised the miraculous, reducing Jesus-the-mystical-Christ to a figure of American agrarian decency and commonsense virtue; in other words, the kind of skeptical, fair-dealing individual landholder whom he regarded as the backbone of the new republic.

Similarly the English writer and Christian philosopher Iris Murdoch struggled with what she believed was the stubborn and futile insistence of Christianity on the literal rather than the figurative truth of its myths, the Virgin Birth and the Resurrection. The Christian duty to believe "six impossible things before breakfast" was, she feared, helping to efface the essential: Christ's ethical vision, that we must love one another. She wanted Christianity as a non-supernatural religion, with Christ the Buddha of the West, a man who became enlightened and whose life – in itself – was a kind of teaching. This reflects the rationalist in Murdoch, who felt humanly drawn to the hero of the Gospels but, like Jefferson, could not accommodate what she perceived as persistent traces of primitive magic and superstition.

The cognitive scientist George Lakoff writes about the psychological underpinnings of two different models of Jesus: Jesus the saviour and Jesus the teacher. The former belongs to a fundamentalist model that conceives of the human community as a patriarchal family in which "male headship" and stern discipline are biblically authorised as the natural and good state of things because they reflect, on earth, a judgmental and punitive Judaic God. This is what Lakoff calls the strict-father model and what others describe as fundamentalist or black-letter religion. On this model, Jesus the saviour is necessary because we are inherently wicked and can only be redeemed (literally) from sin by his extraordinary sufferings.

Jesus the teacher, on the other hand, offers a nurturing ethic that will make us better and more fulfilled individuals *on earth* and in a way that contributes to the general happiness of all. This Jesus Lakoff describes as "nurturant" and he tends to be invoked as the basis for a more liberal Christianity that focuses on the primacy of individual conscience in the personal sphere, and care and compassion for the other – social justice – in the public. Many Christian positions are a somewhat confused blend of the two, with varying degrees of theological coherence.

Even among the fundamentalists, we find personalised representations of the Jesus *imago*, and no more graphic example of this exists than the Jesus of Mel Gibson's *The Passion of the Christ*, so clearly a product of its time. Despite the very interesting attempts at authenticity – a soundtrack in Aramaic, for example – this is a Jesus steeped in violence, brutality and sadism to a degree that some critics have described as verging on pornographic. This is a Jesus whose contemporary *imago* is here "produced" by the *Lethal Weapon* culture and has marked similarities to the paranoid narratives and hero figures of *Lethal Weapon* and *Braveheart*, tales of persecution and salvation that are about retribution and punishment rather than love and forgiveness. It's a Jesus that tells us more about Mel Gibson and the culture of violence in late twentieth-century mass media than it does about the Jesus of the Gospels, just as the Jesus of the musicals *Godspell* and *Jesus Christ Superstar* was a gentle hippie who reflected the cultural "flower-power" revolution of the '60s and '70s. And if we accept that the *imago dei* of any culture, in any era, is deeply implicated in the conceptions of the self produced by that culture, how can it be otherwise? This, of course, is to contest directly the fundamentalist view – found in all religions – that the important things never change and that these are enshrined in ancient scriptural injunctions that, despite their origin in a particular culture and a particular context – Hebrew anthropology and a set of commandments issued to a wandering desert tribe – are true for all ages. To argue otherwise is to commit the sin of "relativism".

In Archbishop Jensen's Boyer Lectures we see a new attempt to proselytise a Jesus *imago* not merely for the self but for the nation, a project that is fraught with contradiction and relies on several logical and rhetorical sleights of hand. There are many of these but I will cite only one here, as when Dr Jensen asks of Jesus: "How do you explain his sheer historical importance while denying his divinity?" The answer is that the two have no necessary connection; the very question suggests a firmly applied set of cultural blinkers, since the same question could be asked of the Buddha and the prophet Mohammed, neither of whom claimed divinity.

In his attempts to make Jesus "relevant", Archbishop Jensen seems stranded in a kind of no man's land of his own making. On the one hand he upholds the secular state, and Section 116 of the Australian constitution:

> The Commonwealth shall not make any law for establishing any religion, or for imposing any religious observance, or for prohibiting the free exercise of any religion, and no religious test shall be required as a qualification for any office or public trust under the Commonwealth.

He declares:

> I am delighted by those words. They were added to protect us; they best suit the sort of society in which I would like to live; and I believe that they will actually help the Christian faith flourish best because establishment is the bane of any religion. I want freedom for religion or non-religion, yours as well as mine.

On the other he makes a remarkable claim for the history of the Israelites as a way to fill the void in our cultural mythos. He begins by taking issue with the authors of *Imagining Australia: Ideas for Our Future*. Anzac and Eureka are weak bases for a national myth, he argues: "Even appropriating the biblical history of Israel as if it were our own could be a better option. It has certainly been done before now; think of how the biblical story sustained the American slaves." Given that only a minority of Australians declare themselves Christians, this is an extraordinary suggestion. More deeply, it reveals a poor understanding of how cultures and their symbols evolve, and function.

A mythos of the kind Jensen discusses can only have potency in both the public sphere and the individual imagination if its roots are deep and have come into being through what George Steiner once described as a "ripening of collective emotion". In many cultures a Christian "ripeness" was pervasive in the pre-modern world but is no longer so. In the US a degree of it remains, not least because the national mythos of white pilgrim settlement of the continent has at its heart a religious rationale. In Australia, however, this was not the case. The only collective ripening of emotion, much of it officially nurtured, has been, for better and for worse, the Anzac story, itself a version of the pre-Christian myth of the young male whose blood in ritual sacrifice is required each spring to fertilise the soil. There is more widespread collective and individual feeling about young Australians who lost their lives in war than about the crucified Christ. There is more reverence among young people on their pilgrimages to Gallipoli than can be observed among their dwindling cohorts in the mainstream churches. In the figure of the Anzac, the sacrifice/crucifixion of the young male god – courtesy of C.E.W. Bean – is secularised and personalised into someone's brother, father, son, grandfather or uncle. To some Christians this may well seem like a sad substitute for the real thing, but it also demonstrates how the Christian mythos is only one of many strains of influence in contemporary Australian culture.

"What future does Jesus have among us?" asks Archbishop Jensen. "Are we going to get him back into the national debate about our lives?" This is an odd question for a defender of Section 116 to ask. What necessary role did Jesus ever have in a *national* debate, as opposed to a private and personal one? Jesus could only be more fully in the *debate about nation* if we blur the separation between church and state, and move towards an established church or elements of a theocracy. And even if Australia were a theocracy, and Jesus a central point of reference in political debate, would Christians agree on what that meant in regard to formulating public policy? Dr Jensen takes Catholic politician Malcolm Turnbull gently to task for promulgating a neo-liberal version of individualism in thrall to the tenets of economic rationalism. As it happens, I'm in sympathy with Dr Jensen's political views in this area, but to the non-Christian what is pertinent is that on many political issues Christians cannot agree among themselves. Here, as elsewhere, there appears to be no clear answer to the question "What would Jesus do?" A Catholic politician such as the Minister for Employment and Workplace Relations, Kevin Andrews, cannot agree with his own Cardinal (Pell) and Pontiff on the importance of trade unions. Despite clear and unequivocal messages in Pope John Paul II's encyclicals on this subject, Andrews, a one-time lawyer, has disputed the papal message somewhat in the manner of a shady advocate in a dodgy legal case seeking a technical loophole. The response of the agnostic to this is to feel that if Christians were more consistent in their message, they might be more broadly persuasive in the public sphere.

It has been said that Dr Jensen was disappointed in the response to his Boyer Lectures. He had hoped they would provoke widespread discussion "around the watercooler". In fact they have passed with remarkably little response, even from the most militantly secular pundits in the community who might have been expected to lock horns with their author. The fact is that the Jesus of the Boyer Lectures is a little dry and a little dull, a Jesus who does not reflect the Zeitgeist or fire the imagination. Had he been the star of a six-part rock opera for television mounted by Hillsong there might have been more of that discussion around the watercooler (sandwiched between vehement opinions on Desperate Housewives and the weekend's football games). Meanwhile plans are afoot for a more dramatic representation as part of the Australian Catholic Church's mounting of World Youth Day in 2008. According to a report in the Sydney Morning Herald, which cites "bid documents sent to the Vatican and obtained by the Herald", Hollywood mogul Mel Gibson will be asked to recreate the Stations of the Cross in Sydney's streets, similar to those staged in his film The Passion of the Christ. Gibson's involvement was "something on our wish list" said Cardinal Pell, and intermediaries had "started approaches" to him to mount the pageant. The Herald continued: "The stations would begin with the Last Supper, probably at the Opera House at sunset, and end with the Crucifixion at St Mary's Cathedral" – a scenario so risible that in "imagining" this Gibsonian via dolorosa I suspected some wag at the Herald of making it up (well, the bit about the Opera House, surely?). The response by the then NSW Minister for Tourism, Sandra Nori, that "apart from the obvious economic spin-offs for Sydney, the event would invigorate Australia's religious life" must also provoke guffaws from skeptical readers. First the Gay Mardi Gras and now this. Could there be no end to Sydney's vulgarity?

None of this would be of interest here if it were a matter of merely religious ritual. Recent developments, however, suggest that the traditionally separate spheres of God and Caesar are becoming blurred. The Christian Right in Australia has begun to model its political interventions on those of its allies in the US and to argue for, and promote, a Christian political constituency. Far more than at any time during the Cold War and its holy crusade against communism, Jesus the saviour is now installed as a major figure in the culture wars. Formerly antagonistic elements of the Christian Right have begun to coalesce loosely around what they perceive as a long overdue counter-offensive against secularism. In the face of a rise in the growth and political influence of Islam, democracy must be reinvigorated with a new moral crusade.

## VOTING FOR JESUS

The uneasy dance of religion and politics has long been an issue in Australian public life and the poisonous sectarian disputes of the nineteenth century were uppermost in the minds of the framers of the constitution when they formulated Section 116 in the hope that this would guarantee the new commonwealth a secular state. At any given time religious lobbies work away to influence governments and this is sometimes perceived as sinister, although arguably it is no less or more so than the efforts of other interest groups seeking to influence public policy. Moreover the success of religious zealots in galvanising a hedonistic Australian electorate with a traditional antipathy to wowsers has been mixed, to say the least. Nevertheless, when Peter Costello waved his arms in the Hillsong auditorium and Steve Fielding was catapulted into the Senate, Christian spokesmen were quick to claim that Australia was undergoing a religious revival, though no one thought to relay this information to Pope Benedict XVI. In August 2005, the Pope issued a dire warning: mainstream Christianity was dying out more quickly in Australia than anywhere else in the world.

Perhaps this apprehension accounts for the Vatican's decision to mount the World Youth Day in Sydney. It may also account for the curious recent interventions made by the head of Australia's five million Catholics, Cardinal George Pell. Anglican Archbishop Peter Jensen is at least clear on what it means to live in a secular liberal democracy, but Dr Pell seems confused and in doubt. In a lecture given in October 2004 to the Acton Institute for the Study of Religion and Liberty in the United States, Dr Pell told his audience that liberal democracy is a world of "empty secularism" that is over-focused on "individual autonomy". The problem with democracy, said the Cardinal, quoting John Paul II, is that it is not a good thing in itself; its value depends on the moral vision that it serves, and a secular democracy is lacking in moral vision.

To dismiss a system based on the principles of equality before the law, freedom of conscience, freedom of speech and action, and responsibility for community as lacking a moral vision was extraordinary in itself, but there was more. Pell went on to argue that the essential flaw in this political system is that it is "secular", a virus of godlessness that gives rise to a catalogue of anathemas, including abortion, pornography, IVF-assisted reproduction and stem-cell research. Because of this, democracy is made vulnerable to the forces of darkness, and in particular to the growth of Islam. Secular democracy not only cannot stop the rise of intolerant religion, it in fact contributes to and worsens it.

Dr Pell urged his audience to rethink the meaning of "normative democracy" and, while not prepared to argue openly for "Christian democracy" – this would be too much of a minefield, even for a controversial cardinal – instead came up with a model called "democratic personalism", founded on "the transcendent dignity of the human". By "transcendent" he meant that we need to recognise our "dependence on God" and place this at the centre of our system of governance although this, he asserted, did not constitute an argument for theocracy. But if placing God at the centre of our system of governance is not theocracy, then what is it? How can a democratic government be based on a series of ancient texts handed down as dogma, texts that are not subject to democratic debate in the way that legislation is (or is supposed to be)?

By any standards this was an astonishing statement of political illiteracy, and with it Dr Pell emerged as a front-liner in the current culture wars against secularism. His is a militant posture that sets out to blur a number of distinctions, the most important of which is the distinction between secularism and atheism. Broadly speaking, there are two kinds of secularism: the militant version that is anti-religion per se, and the secularism that conceives of the state as a neutral referee between competing belief systems; the upholder of individual liberty and freedom of conscience (provided that freedom is not harmful to others). This latter is the secularism that most Australians endorse.

To be secular is not to be anti-religion, but to be anti-theocracy. Secular doesn't mean without; it doesn't mean empty. On the contrary, in the context of liberal democracy it means multiple and diverse or, to pursue the spatial metaphor, "full". This was something that the founders of the Australian constitution understood, and they went to some pains to enshrine it in law, even expressly prohibiting the Commonwealth from imposing any religious test for public office. In the words of Federation historian Helen Irving, "Not only did [Section 116] depart from English practice, it went beyond the First Amendment in the US constitution, which only forbids laws establishing a religion or prohibiting free religious practice."

This makes Australia the most secular liberal democracy in the world. But it doesn't mean that we are godless, and this conflation of secular and godless is too often and too glibly made. Liberal democrats have no objection to the individual's faith in God; they simply assert the importance of allowing individuals to find their own way through to that faith in their own way, and in their own time. The dangers of any other route are manifold. That separation of church and state guarantees one of the great civilising achievements of modernity: freedom of religious observance and non-discrimination on the basis of religious faith. This in turn gives rise to freedom of conscience – that's what the word liberal refers to – and a secular democracy, as opposed to a theocratic one, guarantees that freedom. It guarantees that on every ethical issue in the public realm, *a case must be made.*

The culture wars are fought on many fronts, some more available to public scrutiny than others. Whereas Cardinal Pell was at least open in making his case in the public sphere, today's Australian Christian lobby groups, according to critics such as Marion Maddox, have mostly engaged in unacceptably covert operations: they are a kind of fundamentalist mafia whose influence is out of all proportion to the constituency whose interests they claim to represent. In her comprehensive study *God under Howard: The Rise of the Religious Right in Australian Politics* (2005), Maddox presents a strong argument that even as church attendance is dropping, the influence of right-wing Christian lobbyists is growing, and is disproportionate to their representation in the wider community. On Channel Nine's *Sunday* program, Jana Wendt took up this point and put it to federal Liberal member and moderate Christian Bruce Baird that the share of practising Christians in the country's legislatures far outweighed that in the rest of the community, and that given the low rate of church attendance it was hard to make a case for Australia as a Christian country in other than a cultural sense. In other words, who exactly do these Christian parliamentarians imagine themselves to be representing? What evidence is there for a growing Christian political constituency?

As noted, mainstream church attendance in Australia is in decline – a mere 9 per cent of the population attend – except for a 10 per cent increase in the Anglican archdiocese of Sydney. For all the recent razzamatazz, the Pentecostalists represent a congregation of between 160,000 and 194,000 – depending on whose figures you accept – out of a population of twenty million. The number of church-going Anglicans is estimated at around 170,000. Compare this to the number of "no religion" (2,906,000), declared atheists (347,017) and Buddhists (424,839). The Christian-based Family First Party claims to have 2,000 members, far fewer than the average first-grade football club (whose weekend game attendances are also higher than those of the megachurches). Arguably the most distinctive feature of the Christian Right in Australia is not its actual numbers but its proselytising zeal, and when zealots like Brigadier Jim Wallace of the Australian Christian Lobby seize every opportunity to talk up a Christian political revival, this begins to look like a strategy to manufacture the appearance of a Christian "groundswell". After all, such organised public noisiness is guaranteed to bring a certain cheaply won media profile with the potential to become self-reinforcing.

The evidence for an enlarged Christian constituency is supposed to have manifested itself in three ways in the 2004 federal election. The first is the election of two members of the Hillsong Church to the House of Representatives: Liberals Louise Markus, in the western suburban

Sydney electorate of Greenaway, and Alan Cadman, in the neighbouring electorate of Mitchell. Labor had held Greenaway since it was proclaimed in 1984 and former Hillsong employee Markus won it with a 7.02 per cent swing. It's too soon to tell what part Markus and Cadman's religious affiliations and public proclamations of faith played, because their success is part of an overall drift of the so-called aspirational voter in Sydney's western suburbs away from Labor to the Liberals. There is plenty of evidence to suggest that any Liberal candidate would have won these two electorates in 2004 and little to demonstrate conclusively that the Hillsong brand, or any other kind of Christian badging, was decisive in the outcome.

The second manifestation is the entry onto the scene of the Family First Party and the fact that in thirteen marginal seats its preferences were crucial to the election of Coalition candidates. But does anyone imagine that the majority of those who gave their first preference to Family First were not likely to be Coalition supporters in the first place, just as most Greens voters are former ALP voters and continue to preference Labor in federal elections?

The third "Christian" outcome, the election of Steve Fielding, has been talked up in the media with almost revivalist zeal, but the psephological fact is that Fielding's elevation was as much the product of decisions taken by ALP machine-men in Victoria as any uprush of Christian political insurgency among voters. The two states where Family First came closest to electing senators were Victoria and Tasmania. In Victoria the Labor warlords believed, mistakenly as it turned out, that they could finesse the Liberals and the Greens out of the sixth Senate seat and win it for Labor's Jacinta Collins by preferencing Family First. They misjudged the extent of the swing against Labor and in so doing delivered an unlikely Senate seat to Family First (0.1317 of a quota) away from the Greens (0.6157). Family First polled so badly it was outpolled even by the DLP (0.1356) and was not much above Liberals for Forests (0.1289). Fielding's election is a straightforward outcome of the electoral option known as above-the-line voting, where voters tick a single box marked for their preferred party and do not mark in a thought-out preference ranking. In effect this maximises ticket voting and reinforces, in all parties, the power of the party machines to do preference deals and settle scores. These preference deals remain largely opaque to the majority of voters, and in the weeks following the election many Labor voters discovered that through no intention or genuine preference of their own they had elected a Family First senator. Judging by the correspondence columns of the newspapers and the response on talk-back radio they were less than thrilled by this. To see the full extent of this voting phenomenon one need only look at the figures. In Victoria, the ALP won 36.17 per cent of the total vote. Of this, approximately 0.5 per cent was a ticket or above-the-line vote. In other words, the overwhelming majority of Labor voters were voting for Jesus – but did they know it?

The other state in which Family First appeared to be moderately successful was Tasmania. Here Family First candidate Jacqui Petrusma came within 300 votes of being elected to the Senate. But again, an analysis of the figures tells another story. The Greens candidate, Christine Milne, polled almost a quota in her own right: the overall Greens vote was .9302 and Family First's 0.1667. But the Tasmanian ALP had scores to settle with Milne and they set out to destroy her. Thanks to a preference deal with Family First, they very nearly did. Had Petrusma been elected, it would have made a mockery of the system but, interestingly, Tasmania features the greatest number of ALP voters who do not vote above-the-line and who mark their individual preferences all the way down and across the ballot paper. The difference is approximately 5 per cent as compared to 0.5 per cent in Victoria, and this reflects an electorate conditioned by years of voting in the complex state electoral system of Hare-Clark preference voting.

If the emergence of Family First is indeed part of a Christian revival, then it is odd that the executive minds of the party should have gone to some lengths to disguise its Christian character. Family First was founded in 2002 by Andrew Evans, a former National Superintendent of the Pentecostal Assemblies of God churches and now member of the South Australian Legislative Council (Evans' son, Ashley, has succeeded his father as Pastor of the Paradise Community Church in Adelaide). Its federal chairman, Peter Harris, has a prominent role in the Paradise Church and the party's Senate candidates for the 2004 federal election were chosen from within Christian evangelical ranks and assessed via a thorough screening process based on "political potential and personal morality". Despite this, Andrew Evans explicitly denies that Family First is a church party, a disclaimer that has aroused the ire of other Christian groups. The Christian Democrats' NSW director, Phil Lamb, complained that Family First "have not got the word 'Christian' anywhere on their website. I think that is quite deceptive. They are hiding the fact that they are Assemblies of God people." Public broadcaster and Catholic commentator John Cleary was among the more moderate Christians who took offence: "Family First gained their support base through mobilising networks through the Assemblies of God. Yet when they presented themselves to the Australian public, they attempted to disguise that. Now hang on, let's be honest here. You are either a political party that is Christian and are proud of it, or you are a conservative party using Christian networks and trying to disguise it."

As time moved on, however, attempts to camouflage the party's evangelical character were more effectively undone by its own adherents. Here is Tasmanian Senate candidate Jacqui Petrusma: "Family First isn't a Christian party, [although] it's been started up by Christians. All the people running for parliament are Christians, however we see ourselves as a values-based party. Because basically we know we have to be as wise as a snake but gentle as a dove … if we've got to get out there to the world and try and change values, we can't go out there being a Christian party because most of the world will wipe us off." And it didn't help to have Senate candidate Danny Nalliah – a "Catch the Fire" Ministries pastor and No. 2 behind Fielding on the Victorian Senate ticket – hauled into court for allegedly breaching Victoria's religious tolerance law by making statements likely to incite hatred of Muslims (he also issued a religious tract that implored Christians to pray to bring down "Satan's strongholds" in bottleshops, brothels and Buddhist temples). Nor was it a good look when a Family First volunteer in Brisbane made a comment at a pre-polling booth that lesbians like the young and personable Liberal candidate for the seat of Brisbane, Dr Ingrid Tall, should be burnt at the stake along with all the other witches.

ABC election analyst Antony Green estimates that there has always been a Christian vote of about 5 per cent in the Australian electorate but that for a long time this vote has remained static. In order to increase it, the Christian Right, in the new guise of Family First, needed to broaden its appeal: in Green's judgment, "they need another hook, like family values".

Having observed the degree to which the Christian Democrats and Fred Nile had become something of a wowserist joke in Australian politics and failed to rally followers under an overtly Christian battle flag, Family First followed the example of the Christian Right across the Tasman and abandoned a defined Christian political identity. In New Zealand, elements of the Christian Heritage Party and the Christian Future NZ Party re-formed into the United Future NZ Party which, under that country's system of proportional representation, now holds eight out of 120 parliamentary seats. Prior to the re-badging, the two parties were unable to win seats in New Zealand elections, despite "high-profile recruits". Marion Maddox has outlined the many similarities between UFNZ and Family First, including the proposal to vet all legislation for its impact on families, which she describes as "a direct pinch" from UFNZ.

A strategy to win wider community support by downplaying Christian identity has also been successfully pursued in the US by evangelical groups such as Focus on the Family. Local campaign workers are coached in how to avoid speaking "Christianese" that might alert secular voters to a Christian crusade. Instead, a highly generalised set of motherhood and apple-pie terms is deployed, chief among them being "family" and "values". As social commentator Hugh Mackay has noted, it is a discourse which brings "a new darker note" to the word "family", which now becomes a code word for "conservative" and for the virtues of a particular type of family: conformist, exclusionary and scapegoating. Coded discourse of this kind facilitates a religious dog-whistle politics which, in Maddox's words, enables political leaders "to send different messages to different constituencies at the same time". When Peter Costello proclaims to the congregation at Hillsong, "We need a return to faith and values which have made our country strong," he is apparently deploying a form of rhetoric that begs as many questions as it answers, and is valueless as a statement about the real world. What it does do, effectively, is whistle up the fundamentalists.

In other words, it's all about marketing, about forms of sloganeering that are as good as a nod and a wink. The Christian Right have demonstrated that they are masters of marketing in all spheres, and the new Pentecostalists are not above soft-pedalling the harsher aspects of fundamentalism when necessary, to disarm and engage a moderate audience. In a post-election profile in Fairfax's *Good Weekend* magazine, for example, Steve Fielding is described as "reluctant to discuss his spiritual beliefs these days" and concerned to present himself as "just a family man, not a career politician". This is somewhat disingenuous, especially as Fielding emerges in the profile as a politically ambitious individual who served as a local councillor and considered seeking both Liberal and ALP preselection before he sought out Family First endorsement only a few weeks before the election. In the light of this disclosure, the *faux-naïveté* of his public statements – "I don't know exactly what I can achieve, but families will have a voice now" – can be cringe-making.

It is true that unlike many of the right-wing Christian groups in the US, Family First lays claim to a more moderate position on social justice issues. The party ran on a policy of being against the war on Iraq and took a more compassionate line than the Coalition parties – to which it directs its preferences – on refugees. Steve Fielding has expressed skepticism about neo-liberal economics and opposed aspects of the new industrial relations legislation in the Senate as well as the full privatisation of Telstra. How that translates into *Realpolitik*, however, is another matter. When, for example, it became clear that the Nationals' Barnaby Joyce would be endangering the government bill on compulsory student unionism by voting against it, Fielding sided with the government. Before the vote he met with John Howard; when asked if the meeting related to proposed legislation on the abortion drug RU486, he replied: "To be frank with you, today has been very hectic and I can't recall in actual fact what was spoken about." Odd how quickly conversations with the Prime Minister of Australia can fade from memory. Shortly after, the then Education Minister, Brendan Nelson, issued a statement thanking Fielding, "who has put families ahead of all interests". Yet Barnaby Joyce voted against the bill on the grounds that "Families, five thousand of them, are going to be [adversely] affected by this bill. Where is the impact statement for them?" On one bill, the whole "family values" rhetoric had dissolved into a slush pond of meaninglessness.

## MANAGING THE CULTURE WARS

In Australia, as in the US, the campaigns of the Christian Right are conducted on two fronts. There are the debates in the broader public sphere – the so-called culture wars – in which figures like Cardinal Pell are prominent, and then there is the more local politicking of extremist lobby groups, sometimes from the margins, sometimes from within the major political parties. It's in this latter category that two interesting recent cases present themselves.

Let me begin with the campaigns of the Exclusive Brethren. The Brethren are a small Christian sect of only 40,000 members worldwide with a claim to around 8,000 in Australia. The world head of the sect, the "Elect Vessel", Bruce Hales, lives in Sydney. As well as the usual apocalyptic and messianic views that the Brethren share with some other sects, they are notable for their extreme separatism. The use of computers was until recently forbidden to members, along with mobile phones, radio and television. Members are instructed to eat separately from non-members for fear of contamination and to keep contact with non-members to a necessary minimum. They also support a Prosperity Gospel in which wealth is a sign of God's blessing and the poor have only themselves to blame. Like many US fundamentalists they therefore perceive taxes and government welfare as undermining the divine order. But they do not vote. One might reasonably expect such a sect to shun politics altogether, but in the 2004 federal election they spent a considerable amount of money on advertising to support the Liberal Party and in particular to attack the Greens. One of their target campaigns was in the Prime Minister's own seat of Bennelong, where it was feared that Greens candidate Andrew Wilkie might attract a significant number of dissident and anti-Iraq Liberal votes (in the event, though Wilkie polled relatively well, this didn't happen). Many large and expensive advertisements were placed in local and metropolitan newspapers supporting the Liberal Party and attacking the Greens, and the addresses given on these ads were eventually traced to Exclusive

Brethren members and to one of their educational institutions. Exclusive Brethren members also attempted to disrupt Wilkie's meetings in the electorate. In Tasmania a similar campaign was run against Greens Senate candidate Christine Milne.

In the subsequent New Zealand election an almost identical campaign was mounted, with the Brethren spending an estimated NZ$500,000 on anti-Labor and anti-Green leaflets and advertising. Some of these bore false addresses and were later investigated by the NZ Electoral Commissioner, although no prosecutions were made. It was not clear that the New Zealand material originated with the Brethren and their involvement was only detected when one of the Australian Greens noted the great similarity between the Australian and New Zealand leaflets. Enquiries further afield revealed that the US branch of the Brethren had also invested heavily in 2004 election support for George W. Bush and extreme-right Senate candidates like Mel Martinez – of Terri Schiavo notoriety – in Florida. Their most recent involvement, however, was in the March 2006 state elections in Tasmania, where Trevor Christian and Roger Unwin, two rural businessmen who are members of the Exclusive Brethren, authorised and funded an advertising campaign urging people not to vote for the Greens. This included a pamphlet focusing on the Greens' alleged policies promoting sexual deviancy and "ruining Tasmanian families", in particular their support for the recognition of same-sex civil unions and same-sex adoption and fostering – even though these are already permitted in Tasmania under legislation that was put through by the Bacon Labor government. In perhaps one of the most bizarre details of any Australian election, Tasmanian Greens' leader Peg Putt claims that Greens campaign workers observed Brethren leaflets being distributed by men wearing pig masks in order to disguise their identities.

It is in the nature of elections to be something of a bunfight and a propaganda free-for-all and this is infinitely preferable to the alternative, that is, constraints on free speech. Any lobby group is entitled to campaign for its point of view. The sinister aspects of the Exclusive Brethren campaign arise from the covert character of their interventions: the use of dodgy addresses and the attempts to efface their identity. There are issues here of transparency. Then there are the similarities in wording between the Brethren and the Liberal campaign material. After these were made public, the Liberal Party organiser imported to run the Tasmanian campaign, Damian Mantach, admitted to meeting with the Exclusive Brethren before the election but claimed that this was no more than an informal chat and attempted to disassociate himself from the Brethren material in a deft exercise in hand-washing.

In the Greens' view, however, there is a prima facie case for the Liberals' use of extreme-right Christian groups as attack dogs in election campaigns; such groups offer a means of smearing opponents while Liberal leaders can look on from the sidelines. The Greens point to an apparently neat division of labour in the way in which far-right Christian groups went about their pro-Coalition campaigns in the 2004 federal election. Before the election John Howard met several times with David Harris of Family First to broker a preference deal. In the election campaign Family First spent $600,000 on advertising, much of it negative advertising that focused on attacking the Greens, who at that point were looming as a threat to Coalition control of the Senate. The Greens also cite the professional nature of the Brethren material and its marked similarity to Liberal campaign literature, and see signs of co-ordination in the fact that while Family First financed the electronic advertising that targeted the Greens, the print-media advertising came from a group whose religion does not allow them to engage with the electronic media. As an effective division of labour and use of resources, it seems rather too neat. And since the Assemblies of God churches and the Exclusive Brethren have no time for one another, the Greens argue that it's a case of joining the dots: someone must have been at work in the middle.

Skeptics may see in this just another paranoid narrative such as election campaigns unfailingly give rise to, but they must surely wonder at the extraordinary provision, post-election and buried away in the 1,500 pages of the new workplace relations reform legislation, whereby a small extremist Christian sect – guess who? – is given special dispensation by the Coalition from trade union "interference". The precondition that all workers must agree to blocking union entry to the sect's workplaces has been waived. They are exempted from union right-of-entry rules on the grounds of religious conviction, regardless of the views of their employees. If this is not a political pay-off for services rendered, it has the uncanny appearance of one. And how does it sit with Peter Costello's February 2006 address to the Sydney Institute, "Worth Promoting, Worth Defending: Australian Citizenship, What It Means and How To Nurture It", in which the Federal Treasurer delivered his view that groups adhering to extreme ideas and practices that were not consistent with democratic mores should choose to live elsewhere? If I were a moderate Muslim, currently being exhorted to deal with extremists in my own religion, I might feel somewhat bemused by this.

The second model of an extremist Christian lobby is one that operates not from the margins but from inside a political party. The stand-out case here is the long-term role of Christian fundamentalists within the NSW state Liberal Party and their part in the political execution of small-l Liberal leader John Brogden. This coup appears to have been organised by a collaboration between the right-wing Catholic David Clarke – a 58-year-old member of the NSW Legislative Assembly and self-confessed "co-operator" of Opus Dei – and his Pentecostalist confrères.

The demise of Brogden prompted two revealing newspaper pieces on David Clarke by the *Sydney Morning Herald* investigative journalists Robert Wainright and Paola Totaro, in which a senior Liberal party official is quoted as saying of the NSW Liberal Party: "They (the Uglies) control more than 70 per cent of the executive, the Women's Council, the Young Liberals and now, they – and David Clarke – control the leader [Peter Debnam]." In her article in *The Monthly* on the Young Liberals' 2004 annual conference, Chloe Hooper reports one of the moderate delegates as saying: "We've got a national war at the moment between us and the Right, who are now encompassing the religious Right, and we do not have the resources." Another young moderate tells Hooper that the NSW Young Liberals used to be the "jewel in the moderate Liberal crown", but Clarke "kind of got people together to take over". David Clarke's forty-year efforts within the Liberal Party to mobilise against small-l liberalism of the kind Brogden stood for are well documented and members of Clarke's own party claim that he and his extreme right-wing faction are now in the ascendant.

Described as a "shadowy backroom strategist", Clarke started as an anti-communist campaigner in the '60s and, like so many anti-communists after the collapse of the Cold War, focused his attention on the issues of race and morals. He was once a member of the Fifty Club headed by Ljenko Urbancic, a former Nazi propagandist who mounted a vicious campaign against Sydney lawyer and Voyager crusader Edward St John in the Warringah by-election of 1966 for being a "white traitor" and supporting black political prisoners in South Africa. The Fifty Club pursued a strategy of targeting ethnic groups, especially those recently arrived from communist regimes, using them to build branches within the Liberal Party in a process Marion Maddox describes as "fanning, harnessing and exploiting disparate ethnic groups and age-old tensions". Over time these Right apparatchiks came to be known as "the Uglies". When Urbancic's Nazi past was exposed and attempts were made to expel him from the Liberal Party, this move was blocked by a handful of votes, Clarke's being one of them.

One of Clarke's current operatives is staffer Alex Hawke, national president of the Young Liberals. Hawke worked previously for the right-wing Christian and former federal member for Parramatta, Ross Cameron, and is a member of the Hillsong Church. At the time of his resignation and suicide attempt, Brogden accused Hawke of a gutter campaign against him and of releasing the story of his indiscretions to the press.

When asked on ABC Radio National's *The Religion Report* about allegations of Opus Dei branch-stacking in the Randwick–Coogee area, Clarke told Stephen Crittenden: "We welcome people of all backgrounds of goodwill, but they have to adhere to the fundamental core values of our party." That by this Clarke means "fundamental Christian values" is clear from the rest of the interview. When Crittenden puts it to Clarke that, "there is a view that Opus Dei in the past decade or so has been largely unsuccessful in its attempts to infiltrate the Catholic right-wing of the Labor Party in New South Wales, that it's been largely unsuccessful in its attempts to infiltrate the Commonwealth Public Service in Canberra, and that now it's turning its attention, through you, to the Liberal Party," Clarke dismisses this as "a fanciful idea".

At the time of the Brogden affair – a year on from the Crittenden interview – Clarke declined to be interviewed concerning allegations that he had been behind the former leader's fall from grace. Meanwhile Liberal moderate Joe Hockey weighed into the fray, telling journalists, "There should be closer examination of the views of Mr Clarke." Hockey is notable as one of the moderates of the Liberal Party who, in a speech in the federal parliament, declared: "I do not believe, as do some of my colleagues, that it is the role of government to preach and legislate morality. This is not a church and I am not standing in a pulpit. As an elected representative of the Australian people, it is not my role to exclusively impose my values on others … this parliament is not for moralistic crusades." Following on from Hockey, state Liberal MP Patricia Forsythe declared that, "Extremists and zealots have taken over the party." Just one day before this, on ABC TV's *Lateline* program, former Liberal Party member Irfan Yusuf had claimed that Clarke had advocated criticising Jewish people and homosexuals to attract Labor-voting Muslims to the Liberal Party. Mr Clarke released a statement calling Mr Yusuf's claims "outrageous lies".

For someone of my generation who remembers the bitter sectarian divisions of the '50s, the only surprising element in the Clarke:Hawke/Opus Dei:Pentecostalist alliance is the collaboration between Catholic and Protestant in a way that would have been unthinkable in former times – and perhaps this only serves to highlight, post–Vatican II and the development of the ecumenical movement in the '60s and '70s, that fundamentalists in all Christian denominations now have more in common with each other than with their more liberal and progressive church brethren. Both work off a form of attack-dog politics based on a black-and-white ideological position that seeks to demonise the other. They are the back-room boys of the culture wars.

The US case is instructive here because it suggests where, current differences notwithstanding, Australian politics may be heading. Whereas in former times collective notions like "the people" or even the "nation" were central to the rhetorics of democracy, the degree to which political issues have become privatised is reflected in the fact that in both countries – foreign policy issues aside – "the family" is the most powerful metaphor in politics today.

In his *Moral Politics: How Liberals and Conservatives Think* (1996) and *Don't Think of an Elephant* (2004), George Lakoff reflects on this and identifies two models of idealised family structure that constitute a political spectrum: the strict-father (conservative) and the nurturant-parent (Left or liberal). The strict-father model is based on a set of assumptions derived from the traditional family model of the Old Testament and its teachings: the world is a dangerous place, and always will be, because there is evil out there in the form of Satan. Children are born bad, with Original Sin, in the sense that they just want to do what feels good, not what is right. Therefore, they have to be made good. What is needed in this kind of world is a strong, strict father who can protect the family in a dangerous world and teach his children right from wrong. The best way to do this is through punishment. This ultimately creates internal self-discipline and self-reliance which is what is required for success in a dangerous and competitive world.

Thus the strict-father model links morality with prosperity. These values, based primarily on fear, are externalised and projected onto the nation. Welfare is immoral because it gives people things they have not earned – "wasteful spending" – and creates "dole bludgers". It's a politics that thrives in conditions of fear and uncertainty, which it is well placed to exploit: think terrorism, *Tampa* and the old chestnut of Law and Order. Only the strong father can protect us, and it is this traditional model of orthodox male headship (and submissive women) that explains why fundamentalists from different denominations – and often, religions – have much in common.

Lakoff's strict-father argument is not one that is psychologically reductive in regard to religion as such. It does not seek to explain away why people have religious convictions, but to explain why they have certain variants of those convictions and how these relate to their politics, and it goes some way to accounting for the extraordinary heat that Christian Right extremists generate on the issues of same-sex marriage and abortion, issues which seem to agitate them far more than war, poverty, plague or global warming. This, argues Lakoff, is because pro-choice and gay rights campaigns directly contest and undermine the traditional authoritarian father figure and in so doing constitute a threat to the conservative value system as a whole. It is why they are front-line issues in the culture wars.

Over the last thirty years the Christian Right has mounted a campaign to combat what it perceives as the insidious culture of the post-war welfare state and the so-called permissive society arising out of the cultural revolutions of the sixties. This campaign has resulted in what we have come to describe as the culture wars and relies on attempts to re-frame current political rhetoric. Because rhetoric is crucial to public perception, the culture wars become language wars. It might appear that until recently, the proponents of neo-liberal economics in Australia have not felt the need of Christian window-dressing and relied instead on re-framing voter identity in terms of individual "aspiration". But Marion Maddox's research suggests that covert conservative Christian influence has been greater than acknowledged and that in Australia, as well as the US, right-wing Christian pundits have worked successfully to "re-frame" debates out of extremist

"Christianese" into a secularised discourse that operates as a deceptively coded stand-in. This is even more necessary in Australia than in the US where overtly Christian discourse is more acceptable in public life.

In both countries, however, the aim is to appeal to the greatest possible number of electors, for whom overt Christian moralising might be a turn-off, and to re-frame the "moral" in terms of a crudely conceptualised notion of individual economic self-interest. Conservative Christian voters recognise the code – the dog-whistle – while the rest are snowed. And since there is no more effective means of persuasion than the reduction of a complex idea to a simple one, it works a treat. Who can forget Mrs Thatcher's attempt to defend neo-liberal economics by patiently explaining to a television interviewer that the management of an immense and complex national economy was "really no different from balancing the family budget"? On this model, a boatload of refugees is equivalent to a home invasion. In the same groove, the privatised family now becomes the locus of all good, in the face of much evidence to the contrary, while collective entities of civil authority such as "the people" are relegated to inferior status: dated notions from Enlightenment politics that have had their day (Mrs Thatcher: "There is no such thing as society.") There is no more telling instance of this in recent popular culture than the Mel Gibson movie *Signs*, where malign aliens invade the earth and the embattled father – the Reverend Hess – boards up the house to defend his children, alone (Mum is dead) and entirely without the support of community groups or any agencies of civil society which, for the purposes of the movie, simply do not exist – the strict-father position in major paranoid mode.

Within the strict-father model of "family values" politics there are interesting variations. Politicians in office who hold to a strict-father moral position rarely adopt the strict-father style in public lest it appear unattractively harsh. A conservative populist like John Howard, for example, has worked hard to make of himself a consoling father figure, appearing at every possible public ceremony of grief and physically consoling those afflicted. Meanwhile, looking on over his shoulder are his fixers, stern and punitive types such as Nick Minchin, a man who is almost a caricature of the grim-faced, thin-lipped Gradgrinds of the world. Chloe Hooper reports the following exchange during a Young Liberals' debate on abortion:

> Next up is Gareth ... "My great concern," he says [re the anti-abortion speeches that have preceded him] is that the two speakers who have spoken so far have been men." Sitting behind me are Senator Minchin and his ex-staffer David Miles, a right-leaning Young Liberal who is now manager of government affairs at pharmaceutical giant Pfizer.
>
> "What crap!" Minchin whispers. Then as Gareth continues talking about abortion as a women's health issue, Minchin asks: "Is he gay?"

Bob Hawke incarnated one alternative to the strict father: the fraternal mate, a flawed larrikin but good bloke who could be allowed the "sins" of drinking and womanising because these can be forgiven in a mate but not a father. The Hawke larrikin model tended to shrink the public space available for occasions of public piety, but the Howard father model – strict but reassuring – creates a moral space for the entry of figures like Steve Fielding who would once have been laughed out of Australian politics as a sanctimonious wowser, the natural antagonist of the larrikin. Kim Beazley's problem is that he's perceived as a weak version of the strict father, the proponent of a wishy-washy me-tooism who lacks "ticker". To contest the strong father successfully you have to be something else altogether, like Hawke (a mate) or, in Edward St John's famous polemic against John Gorton, a "good bloke".

Australia was once a society built on the fraternal model – mateship, a fair go – but the Hawke era may have seen its last gasp. And at some level, this may already have seeped into the public mind. A major newspaper poll conducted early in 2006 revealed that half of the nation's voters felt that Australia had become a "less fair" society under the Howard government.

The stigmatising of the Centre and Left as anti-family values is a minefield for progressive parties like the US Democrats and the Australian Labor Party, one they have yet to negotiate successfully. They move to the right and still fail to win elections because this is a game they cannot win. To cite a recent example given by Gore Vidal: nobody can compete with George W. Bush in creating an aura of fear and insecurity because to argue within the paranoid narrative is to risk being labelled unpatriotic. The only way to contest it is to step outside the terms of the debate, as Franklin D. Roosevelt did during the Great Depression when he campaigned on the slogan: "The only thing we have to fear is fear itself." In a recent column in the *Australian*, Michael Costello expressed exasperation at the media mantra that Labor had "run out of ideas". He pointed to the number of thoughtful books on innovative policy published over the last fifteen years by members of Labor caucus such as Lindsay Tanner, Craig Emerson, Wayne Swan and Mark Latham. Where were the comparable books by Coalition politicians? Costello's question misses the point. Labor politicians may well have good ideas and good programs but, in George Lakoff's terms, they are failing to re-frame the public debate and its rhetoric. They talk about "tax relief" as if it were a neutral term. They have yet to re-frame the public debate on their own terms. This is why when Beazley and Rudd talk we say they are prolix, or "boring".

At the same time, certain issues have an inherent potential to stymie the extreme-right agenda, and foremost among these is abortion. So crucial is the pro-choice position to women's experience of themselves in the postmodern world that it continues to defy attempts to take us back into the past. No amount of strategic framing qua family values – and the selectively tuned "pro-life" slogan – has succeeded in altering this fact, as the RU486 debate demonstrated. Anyone who fears or hopes that we are in for a wave of new repression need only look to the unprecedented collaboration, across party lines, of women politicians on the RU486 debate. The Australian parliament has not seen the like before, nor such a clear female/male divide on a piece of legislation.

Attempts by the Right to promote abortion as a wedge issue simply have not worked, despite the fact that it serves as a stand-in for strict-father morality in general. Reporting for the *Age*, Michael Gawenda recently expressed amazement that given the enormous ills of the US – Hurricane Katrina, a crumbling health system, the mess in Iraq – the hot issue everywhere he went was abortion. It seemed, he said, to make no sense. Well, on the rational plane, no, but if we see it as one of the great fault-lines of the extreme-right political position, then it makes perfect sense. Many liberal Christians oppose abortion but do not regard it as the domain of the state, and in this they retain the support of the majority of moderate voters for whom there is no going back – to the backyard, that is. It explains why a contender for the Liberal leadership like Peter Costello must make an artfully equivocal speech on RU486, in effect having two bob each way, while Howard publicly distanced himself from the extreme Right's rhetoric while voting with them on the bill. Even the new Pentecostalists are prepared to "re-frame", that is, soft-pedal on the issue of abortion when attempting to make their sell to a broad public audience. They know that initially, at least, they must tread softly if they are to build up their base. Here is a passage from the *Good Weekend* profile on Steve Fielding:

> The party is against same-sex marriage, stem cell research and euthanasia. But *Fielding himself seems anything but a hardline moralist*, telling me that he is in parliament to represent families of all configurations, not just the standard mum-dad-and-kids, and that he isn't interested in telling others how to lead their lives. Officially, Family First disapproves of abortion, but Fielding says, "It's difficult for women. It's a very difficult decision and one that I wouldn't like to have to face." (my italics)

Compare this to Fielding's active opposition to the RU486 bill. On his website he makes pointed reference to the number of ALP members, as compared to Coalition, who voted for it and lists them by name, presumably so interested voters can be sure to know whom to vote against next time.

Hillsong's Pastor Brian Houston, too, was on the soft-sell trail for the liberal audience of ABC TV's *Australian Story*: "In the church we can point the finger so easily. On the subject of abortion, I'm pro-life. But in a way I'm pro-choice as well, because I believe in the sanctity of life and I believe that life begins at conception. But I also believe that ultimately human beings have to make their own choices, and I ultimately can't tell you what you should do. I can only give you the parameters that I believe." And I can't help wondering what Hillsong member Alex Hawke would make of that. At the Young Liberals' national conference in 2004, he told writer Chloe Hooper: "It's [abortion] going to be back, probably bigger and better."

What the RU486 outcome demonstrates is that all politicians, even the preachifying Christians, have to keep their eye on the moral middle, a moderate mass of voters that belies the fundamentalists' "Moral Majority". The war of propaganda is what counts, but moves that might actually alienate the moral middle are another matter. And there's another problem. The unpleasantness of the tactics deployed by the religious Right of the NSW Liberal Party has tended to create an aura of nastiness around the protagonists and their newly installed leader, the unattractively austere Peter Debnam, who does not appeal to voters and appears to have given the state Labor government a new lease of life. So far it looks to be more effective for the Christian Right if extremist lobby groups operate outside the domain of the Liberal Party's factional politics so that party leaders can, in the manner of Pontius Pilate, wash their hands of the uglier aspects of negative campaigning while reaping the benefits at the ballot box – the Exclusive Brethren strategy.

## STILL THE MAIN GAME

What precisely do the "Christian" political lobbies stand for and what is their political scorecard to date? Despite all the colour and movement of the Pentecostals, all the clapping and swaying and the number of CDs to hit the charts, the traditional churches are still the main religious game in town. Their attendances may have plummeted, but their hit rate as institutionalised lobbies in the arena of the public purse has gone from strength to strength. Their successes and failures tell an impressive story of influence and calculation.

When focusing on social justice, the mainstream churches have advocated a softening of government policy on refugees, especially in regard to the incarceration of women and children. They have opposed the war on Iraq and spoken out against the new industrial relations legislation as inequitable and harmful to family life. But in all of these areas they have met with a singular lack of success, brushed aside by a government that has accused the bishops of meddling in areas beyond their expertise.

Where the churches have been markedly successful is in lobbying for an economic agenda that is straightforwardly about maximising government funding of the churches' own infrastructures through tax exemptions, along with direct subsidy in the areas of education and welfare. This is a kind of socialising of church costs that relies on a canny electoral blackmail that has nothing to do with moral crusades. So successful has this campaign been that in the eyes of its fiercest critics, like Max Wallace of the Australian Humanist Society, it has engendered a back-door dismantling of the boundaries between church and state. Some argue, too, that it has had a corrupting effect on the large welfare/charity businesses that the churches now run.

There has always been a tendency among militant secularists – whose position tends to the view that all religion is iniquitous – to go into downward spirals of moral panic about any incursion of religious sentiment into politics, but such incursions are unavoidable. In a free country religious lobbies have a right to speak out and it's how these incursions are managed in a democracy that counts. It's here, in the area of public subsidy to church operations, that the contribution of the religious lobbies to manifest social inequity is most evident, especially in regard to the privileging of wealthy church schools. All the rhetorical fire-and-brimstone may be about abortion and homosexuality, and to a lesser degree euthanasia and stem-cell research, but the real deal is who gets what from the public purse. If this seems an unduly cynical position, look at the outcomes to date. Despite the fact that the ALP espoused policies that were closer to the publicly stated positions of the churches on almost every position – Iraq, refugees, industrial relations, social welfare – this was not enough of a moral incentive to override the perceived threat to church finances, and in the 2004 election the bishops spoke out against Labor on the basis of Latham's policy of reducing state subsidy to the wealthiest of the church schools.

Meanwhile the Coalition parties remain largely untroubled by arguments over church and state (give or take a Joe Hockey or an Amanda Vanstone). That many of the Coalition leaders have genuine religious convictions is not in doubt, but this only makes it easier for them to trade in the religion market to optimise their electoral profits. They play the Christian lobbies in an artful and cynical way, using them for political purposes where convenient – state aid to church schools, Mark Latham's atheism, family values and Family First preferences – and rebuff them when they are not. Howard's dismissive response to statements on social justice from Cardinal George Pell and Anglican archbishops Philip Aspinall and Peter Jensen have been too well documented to need rehashing here. As with the churches' opposition to the war in Iraq these eminent clerics were dismissed as naive interlopers out of their field of expertise. Where they do not suit the Howard agenda, the churches are hung out to dry: Howard sucks up the moral conservatism and spits out the rest. Liberal Catholic priest Frank Brennan SJ describes Howard's policy as "cherry-picking the bishops". He writes: "A majority of John Howard's senior Cabinet ministers are now Anglicans or Catholics. They wear religious affiliation on their sleeves more readily than did the senior ministers of the Hawke and Keating governments. And yet they have pursued policies on asylum seekers and the Iraq war contrary to the position adopted by most of their church leaders."

Where does this leave the Australian Labor Party? Largely in response to the emergence of Family First, Labor's Kevin Rudd has made efforts to establish himself as a spokesperson on the Christian Labor view and, in Lakoff's terms, to re-frame the public debate on the Christian message as nurturing not punitive – the social justice gospel. On 8 May 2005, Rudd "came out" on ABC TV's religion program *Compass* in an interview with Geraldine Doogue. "My fear is that Christianity will become identified with the Liberal Party," he said. "I've got a responsibility for the tradition of Christian politics that I come from." Rudd cited the early Christian influences in the formation of the Labor Party, where Methodists especially were strong, and the long European tradition of Christian socialism. "Up until now we've seen religion as a private matter," but now Christians in the ALP "have to stand up and be counted."

Rudd believes Family First preferences cost the ALP three to five seats in the 2004 election and claims that at no time did Family First offer the ALP a chance to negotiate for its preferences. In response he has convened the Faith, Values and Politics group within the federal ALP's caucus, a group that, according to one of its members, Peter Garrett, is working on "opportunities for real dialogue with people of faith in the coming months". Presumably this will include Family First and the new Pentecostalists. After all, Fielding spoke up against aspects of the industrial relations reforms and the promised family impact statements on all proposed government legislation have not been forthcoming. Given this, it's easy to see why Kevin Rudd might ask of Family First and Christian voters generally: what is it that you get from the Liberals that you can't get from Labor? If there is no hidden agenda in the Family First wing of the Christian Right, why not go with the party with the best record on social justice?

The answer to these questions may be latent in Fielding's current website, the one where he spells out in detail the number – and names – of Labor members who voted for greater public access to the RU486 pill. Yes, it was a conscience vote, but a greater proportion of Labor members voted for it than did those from the Coalition, something that creates a perfect excuse for Family First not to direct its preferences to Labor at the next election. Abortion may only be one issue among many, but one excuse is enough. Senate preferences, in the end, are all that Family First is likely to be able to deliver, and so far they appear to come cheaply. Commentators on the Right rushed to acclaim Fielding's election as the harbinger of a new political force, while commentators of the Centre and Left highlighted his statements on social justice. "IR plans hit wall of Family First" trumpeted the headline in an article by the *Australian*'s political editor, Dennis Shanahan. But in the end Fielding made little difference to the passage of the bill. As a moral corrective to the depredations of neo-liberalism he promises to be a paper tiger. The Howard government has put on a great display for him of its best party manners, but so far he has been ineffectual in the Senate and has scarcely managed to extract small change.

Even so, Labor is treading cautiously. Rudd and Garrett are reputed to have warned members of the Labor caucus against public criticism of Hillsong and to have made overtures to assist Fielding in the Senate on matters of procedure, even where they disagree with him. Sensibly, Rudd doesn't attack Hillsong and the Assemblies of God, a tactic which would merely play into the Right's hands and its attempt to brand the Labor Party as godless (a fate that befell the Democrats in the US in 2004). For now, the important thing for Labor is that Christianity doesn't become identified with the Right in general and the Liberal Party in particular, not just because such an identification undermines Labor but because it's untrue. There are dangers here for the ALP, however, if it allows the attack-dog strategy to panic it into what looks like a policy of appeasement in regard to fundamentalism. If, like the Coalition, it wants to use the Christian Right to keep the Greens out of the Senate at all costs then that is one thing, but to pursue that strategy is to risk losing Greens preferences for lower house seats (as well as the Senate) and to be caught in a possible swings-and-roundabouts operation. The Christian Right have made it clear that one of their primary objectives is to destroy the Greens electorally, not just because of the moral crusade on issues like same-sex unions but because, as one evangelical minister put it to me, the Greens are an alternative religion of pantheism and nature worship that is "essentially pagan".

How valid is the social gospel and how far can it be prosecuted in the political sphere as a strategy of the Centre Left? Is it, as Rudd argues, a path to social justice, something that might legitimately be re-introduced into Labor's side of the public debate? Certainly it has its theological rationale among so-called spiritual progressives and one of its more interesting proponents is the publisher of the Jesuit monthly *Eureka Street*, Andrew Hamilton SJ. In his favourable review of Marion Maddox's *God under Howard*, Hamilton offers a specifically Christian critique of the current "family values" rhetoric. "Broadly speaking," he writes:

> there are two accounts of what is central in Christian life. The first emphasizes the domestic sphere as the place of fidelity, with the result that domestic relationships and their emphasis on personal honesty, faithful and controlled sexuality, and respectful child raising, have the central place in their ethic. The family is the household of God. The second account emphasizes the following of Jesus in his mission to the excluded and the stranger. Kindness to strangers, and particularly to those whose dignity is most assailed, will be paramount. Family will be regarded with some suspicion, as it is in Mark's Gospel, because preoccupation with family so easily distracts from the universal and radical following of Jesus.

And:

> These two emphases are held together with some tension in Scripture. The challenge to churches is to hold them together so that both domestic and public virtues are given full weight.

This is a critique of fundamentalism expressed with courtesy and moderation, but there is no mistaking its thrust.

Labor skeptics, however, will remain dubious about the value of importing any kind of theology into political debates. They may prefer to consider the words of Justice Michael Adams of the Supreme Court of New South Wales, a former member of the Uniting Church (NSW Synod) Board for Social Responsibility and, from 1996 to 2005, chairperson of the NSW Law Reform Commission. In a long and impressively detailed paper delivered to the Inaugural Australasian Christian Legal Convention in 2001, Justice Adams argues that almost every major reform in modern history – including the much-vaunted Christian opposition to slavery – was opposed by both the organised churches and a majority of individual Christians. At the very least, Christians were heavily divided. In surveying humane changes to the law over four centuries, he writes:

> [It] seems impossible to escape the damning conclusion that the Church contributed almost nothing to the cause of justice, let alone kindness ... I do not think it can be seriously contended that any substantial legal, social or political advance, even in the modern era, has been marked by a Christian consensus, with the possible exceptions in the USA of the extension of civil rights to Afro/Americans in the 1960s and 1970s and the changes to the Australian Constitution concerning indigenous Australians in 1967.

Citing a long list of instances, including the relations between the church and the National Socialist state in Germany, the role of the churches in apartheid South Africa or in the south of the US, or the failure of the Serbian Orthodox Church to take a stance against the atrocities committed by Serbians in Kosovo, Justice Adams concludes that the churches, as such, have generally reflected the dominant notions of the societies in which they operated, "whether they were brutal, cruel, acquisitive, irrational, unjust or (latterly) liberal". What then is the role of the church in law reform? asks Justice Adams, and concludes:

> I think that it can do little else than not stand in the way ... In the end, there is no reason to suppose that the Church will try to defend that which it never helped to create, a liberal democracy governed by the rule of law, for all that individual Christians might do so. In this context, the concerted attack on secular humanism by significant elements of both Catholic and Protestant Churches, though often in ignorance, should be seen as especially sinister.

This is a startling conclusion for a man who is an active Christian and respected elder of a major church.

Meanwhile, stand by for more talking-up of a Christian revival as part of the ongoing culture wars. For any conservative politician in a liberal democracy, the art of religious wedge politics may in the end prove to be a giant finesse of the electorate's gullibility; to talk big and do relatively little. In the culture wars the most telling political art is that of propaganda – to succeed in framing the debates in your terms while artfully exploiting the gap between the rhetoric and the reality. It's a lesson not lost on either the Liberal Party, or on those in the ALP, such as Kevin Rudd and Lindsay Tanner, who are out to re-frame the "faith and values" debates on more neutral terrain.

In the meantime, people in the community will go about their moral adjudications as they always have, on the basis of liberal humanist values and without need of instruction from the Christian Right. Nothing is more annoying to non-Christians than the Christian presumption that without religion, morality would cease to exist. With the incursion of Family First into national politics these people are now both alert and alarmed. If a fundamentalist groundswell does gain momentum, one thing is certain: it will eventually generate its own reaction.

## CODA

In the final stages of my research for this essay I walked across the campus where I was then working and passed by a booth manned by members of the Evangelical Students Union. I stopped and asked for some information, and the fresh, eager young faces offered me a small booklet on the Gospel of Mark. The cover of this booklet had a large iron-grey nail pointing down into a lurid red splatter of blood. *Nailing Jesus Through the Gospel of Mark* it said, and immediately the writing teacher in me wanted to remonstrate with them over their ambiguous phrasing. Instead I asked if I could speak with them some time. In due course arrangements were made and three students in their early twenties joined me in a colourless seminar room to talk about what is and is not a salvation issue, and whether or not it's likely to affect the way they vote.

Before our meeting I read up on the EU literature and websites and found that the EU is an interdenominational group with a strong core of fundamentalist teachings and an upfront emphasis on "the universal sinfulness and guilt of humanity since the Fall, rendering men and women subject to God's wrath and condemnation". There was also a strong emphasis on commitment to "recapturing 'pure' Christianity", of going back to the Bible for a "recovery of Christianity in its original form", in contrast to other movements that "prefer to trust subjective experience, or tradition, or human philosophy as the final source of authority". It didn't sound like the kind of thing you would expect to flourish in a university that is open to new research and new knowledge but all three of the students who met with me – two young women and a young man – were intelligent and engaging and showed signs of thinking for themselves. They read their Bible almost every day and used it as their fundamental source of authority, which sometimes meant that they differed with their priests and ministers on certain points – as to the validity of infant baptism, say – if they could not find what they regarded as sufficient justification in scripture. Their skepticism about ritual and the liturgy (baptism, for example) is characteristic of evangelicals, as was their general scorn for the new Pentecostalism of Hillsong and the megachurches. (When I asked them about Hillsong, they were wary of sounding too negative but the looks between them said it all.) All three were opposed to women playing leadership roles in the church – "it doesn't reflect the model that is described in the New Testament and it doesn't reflect the model of order that is described in the creation account" – and they did not think it right for women to have "any kind of spiritual authority over men". They admitted, though, to a "range of opinions" on this subject among other evangelical students and felt it was good that they could debate it "and still accept someone else's opinion and know that it is still not a salvation issue". They seemed anxious that I should not perceive them as hardline bigots who offer up what their website refers to disparagingly as "download evangelism".

But if women clergy is not a salvation issue, I asked, why is it that so much time and energy is expended on it in the mainstream churches? At this they gave a kind of collective shrug and said that at the moment this wasn't much within their own experience. Given how strong-minded the two young women clearly were, and the leadership potential they appeared to have, I couldn't help wondering how this issue might translate for them in later life.

We pressed on with the "difficult questions". Yes, they were opposed to sex before marriage. They were also united on the undesirability of abortion. The young man was more vehemently opposed to it than the two young women, who were troubled by the complexity of the issue, yet he had the grace to be slightly apologetic about his own vehemence: "I suppose I'm sounding like an oppressive male here." Regardless of their differences in emphasis, all three expressed a heartfelt wish never to have to face the dilemma in their own lives. But in any case, abortion, like women clergy, was not a "salvation issue".

I asked them the question I had asked the Hillsong girls about a good and virtuous person being condemned to everlasting hell and was told, by the somewhat abashed young man, "Since the Fall we are all sinners. I think it's completely fair for everybody to go to hell and in a way unfair that I don't go to hell. But it's a grace that God chose to give me ... and that's God's decision." On the question of the exclusive Christian claim to salvation all three were unequivocal.

And what about politics? Two of the three had never heard of Family First or of Steve Fielding. The young man had heard of Fielding but didn't realise that he had been elected. None of them thought it important. The young man said: "I am a child of the Reformation. Religion is religion, politics is politics. If politics is about representing people, I don't think it's a good thing to have a huge representation in politics when most of Australia isn't Christian. I don't think it's good for Christians to impose their beliefs and their way of life on other people." The two girls appeared to agree, although not as emphatically. Maybe they just hadn't had reason yet to think about it much. It would be interesting to see them in debate with an Alex Hawke.

Much of the time I found the company of these young Christians charming, so their unforgiving view of homosexuals came as a shock, even though I knew enough beforehand to expect it. Still, this is an area of Christian faith that I find truly monstrous. As a pro-choice woman I might be expected to be more affronted by the fundamentalist opposition to abortion, but in fact I understand that position. I don't share it, but I understand it and I respect it. The hatred of gay men and women, however – amounting in some cases to a veritable mania – is something I find genuinely baffling. I have put it to many Christians that being homosexual is not a choice, that it is a given, something in the homosexual person's nature that is of the essence, just as being male or female is. Given that, are they not God's work as much as any of us? When I put this again to my young evangelicals, they are stony. As one puts it: "It's very clear that in the perfect creation, in the beginning, in Eden, there is no homosexuality and after humans rebelled against God then homosexuality comes in, so I see it as a sin and something God judges."

Did any of them have gay friends?

Yes, one of the girls had a close gay friend who, at the age of twenty-one, knew that she must resolve to be celibate for the rest of her life. "She's found that really, really difficult ... but God's spirit works within to change you."

To change what He made in the first place?

Again they look at me stonily, and then the young man intervenes: "It's no worse than being a thief or other kinds of sin. I wouldn't make a case for it being especially bad in that sense. Sin is sin."

And there we have it, the shock of the literal; the unbridgeable chasm between the fundamentalists and the rest. There is a very straight and uncomplicated path between the Garden of Eden and the Garden of Gethsemane and it is achieved at the expense of a great deal of bush-bashing on the textual plane. No allegorical or metaphorical readings here; no ambiguities arising out of disputed translations or readings of context.

There is another uneasy moment when I ask about their personal spiritual practice, about prayer and contemplation. Somewhere in the general conversation I suggest that I am attracted to the Muslim practice of stopping for prayer five times a day, that in a world where we are all a little stressed and overworked it seems to make sense to have a few structured moments of peace. I even venture a joke about how, with the disappearance of the tea-break and the lunch-break, the prayer-break might be a new way of keeping our nervous systems from meltdown. But with the very mention of the word "Muslim" a chill comes into the room, and both quietly and economically it is made clear to me that nothing that is Muslim could possibly be of value.

But the most startling moment in our conversation comes when I ask these three young people about their upbringing. Two of the three have been raised as Christians. The young man had gone to a church school and offered the rueful opinion that "you get persecuted more for being a Christian at a Christian school" and it was "harder to stand up as a Christian" than it would have been in a government school where he suspected there was a more of a culture of toleration for diversity and difference. Despite being at a church school, as an evangelical he felt himself to be in a scorned minority and was heavily "teased" about his commitment, "not that I ever went around preaching at anyone".

The young woman has another story altogether, one that I want to leave in her own words. "I was thirteen when I, well, 'came to the faith' I guess, is the tacky cliché for it. I definitely didn't consider myself a Christian as I was growing up, but at the age of thirteen I was suicidal and depressed, and really, really upset, and at one point contemplating suicide. And I had a vague recollection of someone telling me that suicide is the ultimate sin. You can't ever be forgiven because you don't have any time to repent after you die, and so I'm like, oh, that's not good. Okay, God, I'm really, really upset, I'm in pain, I don't like how my life is, I'm going to kill myself. If you're real and I kill myself, then I'm going to go to hell. If you're real and you don't want that to happen, you need to do something, clearly here, so that I know you're real. And so I tried to slit my wrists – and the knife didn't cut. So I went into the kitchen and sharpened it, and it still didn't cut. And I went, 'Okay, I believe, I'm understanding.' My arm wasn't bleeding because God wanted me to live. And at that point I went and found a Bible, there was one in the house, in the bookshelf, and I just opened it at random and the first thing I read was Psalm 139, which is 'You are beautiful, you are wonderfully made, I created you, I know all the hairs on your head ...'" Her voice trails away.

The other students look stunned. They haven't heard this before. They are moved. I am moved. I look at this girl, and she looks back at me, and for the first time there is a painful recognition between us, a recognition that has nothing to do with dogma. There is a mystery at the heart of our being-in-the-world and sometimes we experience that mystery directly and affectingly. This young woman, in her dark night of the soul, opens the Bible at random and what lies there awaiting her? An affirmation of her worth; not just her worth but her beauty. The atheist would say this was a coincidence but if it is, then human experience over the years testifies to thousands of these "coincidences". I don't believe in coincidence, having observed too many of a profound nature, and in any case I am not an atheist and I do believe the spirit moves in us. But while I respect the experience, I cannot accept the dogma and the cultural baggage that come with it, because just a few minutes before these same intelligent, graceful young women, and man, have told me that their lesbian friend should remain celibate all her life because she is, in her essential nature, not beautiful but perverse.*

I look at these young adults and they truly are wonderfully made, and I wish we could agree on more; could meet up on some other, wordless, plane, free of dogma, free of all this stuff. But unhappily, for me at least, we are here, now, across the divide of the literal Word. Still, the Word notwithstanding, I am left with the impression that some commonality remains. If in their mature years they are still "children of the Reformation", then we will continue to share a commitment to that great humanist project, a secular liberal democracy in which freedom of conscience is paramount; in which the mysterious unknowability of someone else's faith is respected and protected, but not at the expense of those for whom that mystery is of an altogether different order. It may be that I would choose to emphasise the "secular" in that formulation rather more than these young people, but for now the system embraces us in a broadly consensual understanding of civic virtue. I hope that consensus holds.

---

* In response to this, the ESU student whose attempted suicide story is told here and to whom I sent a copy of my text, wrote: "I believe my gay friends, and all homosexual people, are beautiful. I believe their homosexuality is perverse. In my mind these two statements are not contradictory."

# SOURCES

| | |
|---|---|
| 11 | "only 15 per cent": Jill Rowbotham, "Life's on-call butler: how teens view God", *The Australian*, 4–5 March 2006. |
| 11 | "in another and larger study": Jill Rowbotham, "Self is the new Bible for the young", *The Australian*, 20 January 2006. |
| 11 | "personal crisis in his faith": Margaretta Pos, "When faith can't fulfill", *The Mercury*, 22 April 2000. |
| 16 | "We're living in the last days": Franklin Graham interviewed by David Neff and Timothy Morgan, "Jesus Freak", *Christianity Today*, 18 November 2002. |
| 17 | "Pentecostal church ... flamboyant and out there": *Encounter*, ABC Radio National, 12 June 2005. |
| 18 | "Out went 200-year-old hymns": "The glue of society", *The Economist*, 14 July 2005. |
| 18 | "importance of 'belonging'": *Encounter*, ABC Radio National, 12 June 2005. |
| 19 | "debuted in the top four of the ARIA charts": *PM*, ABC Online, 13 July 2004. |
| 20 | "nothing new in the showbiz phenomenon": Gary Bryson, "It's a God Thing: The Rise of the Megachurch", *Encounter*, ABC Radio National, 24 April 2005. |
| 21 | "re-branding of Christianity": Dr Carole Cusack, "Hillsong's True Believers", *The Sydney Morning Herald*, 7 November 2004. |
| 22 | "the Hillsong 'brand'": Brian Houston, *Australian Story*, ABC TV, 1 August 2005. |
| 23 | "Megachurches represent a degraded theology": Bill McKibben, "The Christian Paradox: how a faithful nation gets Jesus wrong", *Harpers Magazine*, August 2005. |
| 25 | "Christianity as being for losers": Roy Eccleston, "The atheist who's selling Jesus", *The Australian*, 30 September 2005. |
| 26 | "tax-free status": Adele Ferguson, "God's Millionaires", *Business Review Weekly*, 26 May 2005. |
| 27 | "misuse of large federal grants": Jonathan Pearlman, "Hillsong denies bribe allegation", *The Sydney Morning Herald*, 23 December 2005. |
| 27 | "indigenous development grant ... providing office for church staff": Ean Higgins, "Hillsong spent grants on its staff", *The Australian*, 13 February 2006. |
| 27–28 | "church-goers ... still rate at scarcely above 10 per cent" and "attendance in |

| | Australia declined": from the National Church Life Survey, 2001. The full survey can be viewed at <www.ncls.org.au/default.aspx?sitemapid=93>. |
|---|---|
| 30 | "trusted the Word more than the Image": Diana L. Eck, *Darsan, Seeing the Divine Image in India*, Anima Books, USA, 2000, p. 20. |
| 31–32 | "'I don't want to talk about the institutional church'": Peter Jensen, *The Future of Jesus*, Boyer Lectures, ABC Books, Sydney, 2005. |
| 33 | "Cultural icons, like U2's Bono": Julia Baird, "The Way Cool Messiah", *The Age*, 23–4 December 2005. |
| 33 | "'[Jesus] becomes a battler'": "The Way Cool Messiah", *The Age*, 23–4 December 2005. |
| 36 | "[Jensen] begins by taking issue": Macgregor Duncan et al., *Imagining Australia: Ideas for Our Future*, Allen & Unwin, Crows Nest, 2004. |
| 38 | "Mel Gibson … to recreate the Stations of the Cross": Linda Morris, "Film star offered role in Pope's visit", *The Sydney Morning Herald*, 6–7 August 2005. |
| 40 | "the Pope issued a dire warning": Desmond O'Grady, "Pope singles out 'faithless' Australia", *The Age*, 22 August 2005. |
| 41 | "secularism that most Australians endorse": Newspoll Survey, 3–5 February 2006. The full Newspoll survey results can be viewed on the website of the NSW Humanists, <www.hsnsw.asn.au>. |
| 42 | "'Not only did [Section 116] depart from English practice": Helen Irving, "Trespassers in the Name of Heritage", *The Sydney Morning Herald*, 3 June 2004. |
| 42 | "Jana Wendt took up this point": "Hillsong: Songs of Praise – and Politics", *Sunday*, Channel Nine, 3 July 2005. |
| 43 | Statistics relating to church attendance can be found on the World Christian database <www.worldchristiandatabase.org>. |
| 43 | A series of articles in *Business Week* in the US suggested that even in that very Christian country the churches were not in fact growing overall, and even some evangelical groups, critical of the "faddism" of the megachurches, have expressed similar doubts. A Harvard University study found that the number of Americans of no religious affiliation had grown sharply since the mid-'90s, while the membership of the religious Right had remained static between 2000 and 2004. See Steven Waldman and John C. Green, "Tribal Relations: how Americans really sort out on cultural and religious issues – and what it means for our politics", *The Atlantic Monthly*, January/February 2006. |
| 45 | In the April 2006 state election in South Australia, Family First added one member to their upper house numbers for a total of two but were comprehensively outpolled by the No Pokies group – 0.59 of a quota to 2.52 – led |

by crusading lawyer Nick Xenophon. In Tasmania, Family First, re-badged as Tasmania First, was unable to field candidates in all five multi-member electorates and polled pitifully.

46 "The Christian Democrats NSW director, Phil Lamb, complained": Marion Maddox, "God, Howard and evangelical politics", Australian Policy online <www.apo.orgh.au>, 23 September 2004.

46 "'You are either a political party that is Christian and are proud of it'": John Cleary, *Compass*, ABC TV, 1 May 2005.

47 "similarities between UFNZ and Family First": Marion Maddox, "Election 04: God, Howard and evangelical politics", Australian Policy Online <www.apo.org.au>, 12 October 2004.

47 "'a new darker' note to the word 'family'": Hugh Mackay, "Just what is this thing called family?", *The Age*, 12 August 2005.

48 "facilitates a religious dog-whistle": Marion Maddox, "God, Howard and evangelical politics", Australian Policy online <www.apo.orgh.au>, 23 September 2004.

48 Post-election profile of Steve Fielding: Jonathan Green, "Tears and cheers: Family First man's debut", *The Age*, 10 August 2005.

49 "proposed legislation on the abortion drug RU486": ABC Online, 9 December 2005.

51 "Brethren leaflets distributed by men wearing pig masks": "Elusive Exclusive Brethren," *Background Briefing*, ABC Radio National, 30 April 2006.

52–53 "a small extremist Christian sect ... is given special dispensation": *The Religion Report*, ABC Radio National, 5 April 2006, cites page 428 of the new Workplace legislation, Part 9, Division 6, Section 223 of the new Act which, in Stephen Crittenden's words, "allows members of a religious society whose doctrines preclude belief in trade unions, to obtain a conscientious objection certificate to keep unions away from their businesses". See also Mark Davis, "Brethren bosses better armed against the comrades", *Australian Financial Review*, 3 April 2006.

53 "The demise of Brogden": Robert Wainright and Paola Totaro, "A right wing and a prayer", *The Sydney Morning Herald*, 10–11 September, and "Clarke accused of recruiting anti-Semites for Liberals", *The Sydney Morning Herald*, 8 September 2005.

53–54 "on the Young Liberals' 2004 annual conference": Chloe Hooper, "Young Libs in the Chocolate Factory", *The Monthly*, June 2005.

54–55 "about allegations of Opus Dei branch-stacking": *The Religion Report*, ABC Radio National, May 2004.

| | |
|---|---|
| 55 | "Joe Clarke weighed into the fray": Mike Seccombe and Andrew Clennell, "Hockey kicks along Libs' rolling brawl", *The Sydney Morning Herald*, 7 September 2005. |
| 55 | Hockey speech to federal parliament, 21 August 2002. |
| 55 | "advocated criticising Jewish people and homosexuals": Irfan Yusuf, *Lateline*, ABC TV, 5 September 2002. |
| 56 | "strict-father moral position": Malcolm Fraser was an exception: "Life wasn't meant to be easy." Ironically Fraser's policies were more liberal than his image at the time suggested. Mrs Thatcher, on the other hand, made no bones about projecting the female version which is why she was often characterised as the strict nanny of British politics. |
| 59 | "exchange during a Young Liberals' debate on abortion": Chloe Hooper, "Young Libs in the Chocolate Factory", *The Monthly*, June 2005. For yet another version of the strict father, this one in messianic mode, see Frank Robson's profile of Tony Abbott, *Good Weekend*, 14–16 April 2006. |
| 59 | "Australia had become a 'less fair' society": Damien Murphy, "A meaner country, and a good job too", *The Sydney Morning Herald*, 20 February 2006. |
| 61 | "'But Fielding himself seems anything but a hardline moralist'": Jane Cadzow, "Meet the Fieldings", *Good Weekend*, 8 October 2005. |
| 62 | Alex Hawke at the Young Liberals' conference 2004: Chloe Hooper, "Young Libs in the Chocolate Factory", *The Monthly*, June 2005. |
| 63 | "dismantling of the boundaries between church and state": Max Wallace, "Constitutional coup and its consequences", <www.newmatilda.com> , 27 July 2005. |
| 66 | Dennis Shanahan, "IR plans hit wall of Family First", *The Australian*, 11 August 2005. |
| 67 | Andrew Hamilton SJ, "Governments bearing moral gifts", *Eureka Street*, May 2005. |
| 68 | Michael Adams, "Christianity and Law Reform: A historical perspective, with special reference to the criminal law", paper delivered to the Inaugural Australasian Christian Legal Convention, 1–4 February 2001. For the full text of this paper see the website of the Christian Lawyers Society, <www.lcf.pnc.com.au/convention_papers42.htm>. |

# WHAT'S LEFT?

Correspondence

Rebecca Huntley

I finished reading Clive Hamilton's *What's Left? The Death of Social Democracy* on a sunny Easter Sunday afternoon. I laid it down with a deep sigh, feeling both dejected and full of ideas about how to respond. "Why do you continue to care so much about the ALP if it makes you so unhappy?", my husband asked me, not for the first time. "Well," I replied, "because it's important. And sometimes, love isn't meant to be easy."

There is much about Hamilton's contribution to the current debate about Labor that is correct. It's just his conclusion I don't agree with.

Hamilton starts his *Quarterly Essay* with a remembrance of conference past, one in which the Labor Left bristled at his ideas about a policy shift from an emphasis on growth and deprivation to a focus on the social and environmental effects of affluence. Hamilton is right when he says Labor's Left has a strong tendency to be reactive, even conservative, in its approach to policy, one consequence of spending so much of the Hawke–Keating years defending (often unsuccessfully) the status quo. As an active member of the Left faction, I sometimes feel we spend too much time protecting old policy positions with worn-out ideological arguments. This is certainly the case when we look at how the party has tackled – or, more accurately, avoided – the question of affluence.

There seems to be genuine public confusion over whether Australians are "doing it tough" or more prosperous than ever before. At the same time as Hamilton is successfully publishing books like *Growth Fetish* and *Affluenza*, journalist Elizabeth Wynhausen is writing about the working poor in her book *Dirt Cheap*. It seems, however, that both Hamilton and Wynhausen are correct. A minority of Australians – anywhere between 5 per cent and 15 per cent – are living in poverty. Many in this minority are part of an entrenched underclass: people caught in cycles of unemployment, poor education and housing, and abuse of all kinds. The rest of us are enjoying record levels of wealth but not, importantly, wellbeing. In light of the fact that the majority of us are doing quite well, Labor needs to rethink its commitment to the deprivation model.

Interestingly, this attachment to the deprivation model is more rhetorical than actual. Australians living in poverty are not a key constituency for any political party. The teenage mum or unemployed man living in housing commission flats aren't viewed as particularly heroic figures when compared with the coalminer or wharfie of Labor lore. Consider how public housing has fallen off the political agenda, even in the ALP, where a number of parliamentarians spent their childhoods in housing-commission properties. Rather, the talk on the hustings is all about mortgages and interest rates. In its inability to grapple with the new politics of affluence or to deal with the minority underclass, Labor is failing the next generation of Australians, the young people of Macquarie Fields, as well as middle-class teens and twenty-somethings with HECS and mobile phone debts.

Hamilton is right when he points out that the majority of Labor politicians are tentative about seizing on a deeper analysis of consumption. Such tentativeness is out of step with the concerns of so many young Australians. In my research on Generation Y – young Australians now in their late teens and early twenties – I found them to be seriously conflicted about consumerism. On the one hand, they are notoriously enthusiastic and indefatigable consumers. They are a generation for whom consumption is a sport, a hobby, a way of life and, most importantly, a key mode of self-expression. However, I also found that the vast majority of young Australians believe that our society's obsession with consumption and material goods is ultimately destructive. There are high levels of cynicism among Gen Yers about our empty consumer culture and the invasion of the brand into our society. In particular, while young people want money for the freedom and options it provides, most recognise the pursuit of "stuff" cannot provide the basis for a life philosophy. They question the values of a society that equates success with money, especially when that success has a human toll: broken marriages, poor friendships, estranged children. In light of this, I feel Hamilton overstates his case in his comments on "the individualised world". There are mitigating factors at work here, a curb on young people's unqualified embrace of consumption and the market. One of these forces is friendship, an almost romantic belief in the importance and durability of the friendship group. Then there is their reverence for marriage, the desire for permanent and fulfilled family arrangements. Connected to this is their commitment to balanced living, their intent to avoid the workaholism and wage slavery they have observed in their parents. These early impulses, if they persist into later life, have the potential to create an electoral base of support for a political party willing to cultivate a new politics of wellbeing.

Due largely to a perceived inability to develop such a new political vision, Hamilton concludes that we must abandon the ALP as force for social justice and progressive social change. He also revisits what is now a well-worn, albeit accurate, critique of what's wrong with the ALP as a party. This critique was best articulated in a previous *Quarterly Essay, Beyond Belief,* by John Button. Since Labor lost power over a decade ago, we have been treated to countless op-eds, books, essays and speeches describing Labor's malaise, pinpointing our inadequacies and past errors. These dissident remarks circulate against a backdrop of Labor denial. There is now a deadlock within Labor ranks about the way forward. The majority of those in power reject the notion that there are genuine problems. Their energies are directed towards maintaining the present course, hoping that the pendulum will swing Labor's way through force of time, that Kim Beazley will be the Labor equivalent of John Howard, the loser who triumphs in the end. Those calling for reform air their grievances and critiques but rarely, too rarely, offer rank-and-file members any concrete solutions. No one seems willing or able to develop a practical campaign to fix these problems. I don't believe any institution created by people can't be changed by people. But leadership is needed and, unfortunately, sorely lacking among those in power with the desire and capacity to reform the party.

Hamilton comments at length about former federal leader Mark Latham. He observes that when a narrow majority of the caucus elected Latham as leader, it was a brave and bold move in favour of new ideas over old ways. Looking back, the decision to endorse Latham seems akin to the desperation of a woman who hasn't been on a date in years, who says yes to the first promising male who asks her out, fantasising about the engagement before the entrée is finished. We expected too much based on too little. But Latham, for all his faults, offered us (especially Laborites of a younger generation) a peep at an alternative Labor Party, one that attracts candidates like Peter Garrett, that articulates an independent foreign policy, that considers a good public school (rather than a large corporation) to be our most important institution. In Latham's transformation from Labor messiah to stay-at-home psycho, much has been lost. Now anything that smacks of Lathamism is derided in much the same way as was Whitlamism during the early years of the Hawke–Keating government.

Hamilton admonishes those interested in reforming the ALP for focusing largely on structural concerns. He states: "It is pointless debating organisational reform without first debating philosophical renewal." It is certainly easy for debates about reforming Labor to be sucked into never-ending talk about processes and structures. Understanding the rules and regulations of the party – and being able to manipulate them – is a key attribute (along with a penis, it seems) if you want to be a Labor Party powerbroker. Of course, just arguing about structural reform keeps the debate on comfortable footing for the majority of party hacks, who couldn't come up with a fresh idea if their parliamentary super counted on it. However, like so many people outside the ALP's unique culture, Hamilton underestimates the extent to which structure is both an impediment and a facilitator of party democracy and, ultimately, policy development. Structural change is important. I have seen how the party's convoluted and antiquated rules and organisation can stifle debate, prevent involvement from unfactionalised members, undermine democratic principles and divert energy away from discussion and campaigning around ideas. However, the drive to democratise the party's structures has to happen simultaneously with a wider debate about policy and purpose. Hamilton is right when he argues that form should serve content.

Unlike Hamilton, I remain ever hopeful about the ability of Labor to reform itself. On a practical note, I believe it would take less energy to change the ALP than it would to start a new, viable political party based on the principles espoused by Hamilton. I still believe in the capacity of the ALP to heal itself, to change, to face the challenge of an altered political, social and economic climate. It has happened in the past. Under inspired leadership and the support of the membership, Labor has made significant changes: from a national conference of faceless men to an open conference with delegates from all states and territories, from a White Australia policy to government-sponsored multiculturalism, from a party run by a red-faced fraternity to a party supporting sex discrimination and affirmative action laws. Of course, Hamilton is correct when he says that the kinds of changes he is proposing are more fundamental than those just listed (economic and growth imperatives underpinned both White Australia and multiculturalism, industrially entrenched sexism and state-sponsored feminism).

But the development of a progressive politics of happiness and wellbeing as espoused by Hamilton is too important, too urgent a task to be left to some yet-to-be-established minor party.

Rebecca Huntley

# WHAT'S LEFT?

## Correspondence

### Guy Rundle

There's much to agree with in Clive Hamilton's essay: he's spot-on in arguing that the ALP can no longer base itself in a heartland of scarcity, not only for the sake of electoral success, but also for the sake of low-paid workers and those dependent on benefits. A progressive party needs a comprehensive program to address the needs of these groups, but it can't make that the centrepiece of its message to the public. Activists are right to emphasise that this minority is quite a large one – but it is not large enough to command sufficient political heft to counterbalance the broad middle of relatively prosperous consumers, whose support the party must win. If Hamilton's essay does nothing more than hammer this point home further to a few of the more nostalgic members of the shreds of the Socialist Left, the trade union movement and the community sector, it will have done a service.

Nevertheless, I have reservations about both particular and general features of Hamilton's argument. I would suggest that not only is it too pessimistic with regard to the chances of the federal ALP – and the degree to which a federal ALP could have a progressive dimension – but also far too optimistic that the social and cultural dilemmas we face can be solved within the framework of politics as traditionally understood. The paradox, as I hope to show, is only apparent.

God knows, you'd have to be a saint or a masochist to get involved with the federal ALP at the moment. Ten years that should have been devoted to the slow development of a new centre-left/centre-transformational politics have been squandered in blundering between a small-target strategy and single-issue (Medicare Gold) vote bidding. The party is dominated by men – Beazley, Crean, Ferguson – who seem like decent people, but who are living their fathers' lives, without, deep down, any clear idea of why they are there or of the degree to which the world has changed. The ALP has twice made leader a man who has already confessed to having achieved his life's ambition by being a defence minister two decades ago, and whose greatest service to the party would be to vacate the leadership immediately and retire, instead of hoping that John Howard will be found in bed with a dead under-14s netball team or a live Chippendale six weeks before the next poll. Most of the party's vaunted "new breed" are dim-bulb ex-student politicians, and the few genuinely talented new recruits are being sidelined if they lack factional backing. Furthermore … but, well, why recap the essay? Labor is a rag-and-bone shop, and there seems no reason, given current circumstances, to expect victory in the next two federal polls.

But that is given current circumstances, and one of the things missing from Hamilton's essay is consideration of the dynamic nature of the present moment. The transformation of class and income (I'll presume that Hamilton's argument that class has ceased to exist is shorthand) has created a newly prosperous middle band, but it is one dependent on an economy that is overextended both nationally and globally. China – whose purchase of raw materials is funding much of our growth – is a runaway economy that could easily trip up; no one really knows whether its reported growth and earnings are matched by reality or likely to persist. A major reversal, runs on overstretched banks, a recession/depression – such things are scarcely unprecedented. Since a lot of Chinese holdings are in US Treasury bonds, deficit-ridden America would be hit with a major withdrawal of capital, and it would pretty much go from there. Many in the newly prosperous middle band in Australia would then get a reminder that class does exist and that they're in the "working" section of it – when redundancies and cuts in wages and working hours make it impossible to service credit-card and mortgage debts.

Should this occur, Labor would be in prime position to paint the government as wastrel incompetents who sold us down the river of private debt, and thus harvest the anger directed at the government. (It should have been preparing for this for years, by educating the public about the degree to which the government has failed to invest in national development – education, training, R&D, high-end industry development – and allowed the wheels to keep turning on the strength of a Visa card.)

Had Labor done the hard work of stoking the political imagination this past decade, it could be in a position to win power under any set of economic circumstances. As it is, even the scenario outlined above – which economists from across the political spectrum see as feasible – does not guarantee it an inside run.

However, should victory be gained, progressive elements in the party would be revived, and progressive programs implemented. Labor may have to – in fact, must – adopt a centre-right program on big-ticket items such as tax cuts, but labour governments do hundreds of small things that improve people's lives, and in which genuine social change is facilitated. Bill Shorten is right to argue that what Labor needs is "success". As the Coalition in the '80s and '90s showed, and the UK Tories demonstrate today, the simple fact of being in opposition is often enough to make failure a vicious circle.

That should not excuse Labor for its failure of initiative. As Hamilton notes, this failure has its roots in a deep anti-intellectualism within the party – and yet it is precisely a connection between the different parts of progressive politics that Labor has so desperately needed these past years. Compare and contrast the UK Labour Party, which transformed itself through the '90s by extended interchange with think-tanks like Demos – which combined social democrats with former communists of a Gramscian "eurocommunist" stripe to produce a range of new ideas about how a progressive government should interact with social and economic life – and also with writers and thinkers such as Anthony Giddens. The result? When the Tories finally fell over, Labour managed not only to take power but to capture it in a landslide, and to transform the political landscape of the UK. From the left some of that program has to be opposed immediately – New Labour's relentless attack on civil liberties uppermost – but there is no doubt that the lives of tens of millions have been transformed for the better by the myriad of programs that arose from those intellectual conjunctions. Politically, they gave Labour a weapon and a language with which to recapture the political imagination – something the ALP has failed to do and which all progressive parties need to achieve if they are to take power.

Yet here lies the paradox – in the current framework, British Labour is about as good as it is going to get, because we live in a world in which the politico-cultural framework allows no other substantial initiative at the party-political level. I think this is why the program that Hamilton outlines at the end of his essay seems to be both similar to a raft of current ALP initiatives and, I would suggest, also unachievable. It seems, in style and substance, to be a prescription for Scandinavian-style democratic socialism down under. That's been tried in a lot of places and the only one where it works is, well, Scandinavia, where social democratic parties have held power for so long that they have shaped the culture and personality of their nations to such a degree that what would be contentious radicalism in other polities has become commonsense in theirs.

There's no hope of that here, even if we didn't have to contend with a far-right Murdoch press and a right-shifted Fairfax. Even Scandinavia may find it tough to hold onto because the very structures of contemporary Western life undermine the cultural capacity for politics with a collective dimension (and there is a fairly heavy-handed statist dimension to aspects of Scandinavian life). It is not merely prosperity – not the content of social life, but the form of it as created by the dominance of the global media and market – that is rapidly making conventional politics obsolete. Extended media and an extended market now act as the key formative constituents of the contemporary person, who experiences life as "hyperindividualised" – identity springing not from class, church or other collectivities but from the obligation (rather than the choice) to form a self and a world through self-fashioning (conscious and unconscious) in the market and media flux. Acquisition and consumption, therefore, are not simply add-ons – bad habits that can be got over on a mass scale via a new spiritual politics – but are in fact the essence of self-expression and existence within a media-consumer society. The ironic novelty lapel button "I shop therefore I am" is also dead serious. We've now had two generations of the latter, and most people under a certain age don't know any other way to be – and seem, most of the time, to be content enough with it (even if, from another angle, it looks passive, incurious and far from the ideal of the fully human). That is not to buy into the idea that rising generations have "sold out" a '60s revolution, but simply to suggest that major transformations of the cultural framework can rapidly shift the ground under political positions and debates. Hence Hamilton's use of "alienation" is unhelpful – people feel deeply at home in a consumer culture. They also frequently feel anxious, fearful, empty, depressed and panicked, but they accept these feelings as existential features of everyday life. Making visible the connection between a form of social life and its negative dimension cannot be achieved through an appeal to the joys of austerity. It was possible in the '60s – when society was on the borderline between old industrial society and consumerism (and when socialism, the idea that people might democratically control the forces that shape their lives, was on the table) – but not any more. The cultural-social transformation has been accomplished that makes such a world, for the moment, a distant memory of hope.

That goes also for old-style politics. Trade unionism, party membership – for the mass of people these are not merely turn-offs, they are category errors, as out of time and place as if one were to ask them to join the Knights Templars or take ship on a fast clipper bound for China. Hamilton's least useful idea is that we need a new progressive party. Another party? More sitting in draughty church halls, drafting programs, having splits etc.? No. Not going to happen. The Greens are the last progressive party to emerge for the foreseeable future, because they are an organic political expression of a new social class: knowledge producers and administrators. Several more election defeats could see the ALP recomposed as a post-union centrist party, but it would have essentially the same undemocratic, technocratic structure as it has now. The modern political question – market or socialism? – has been resolved in favour of the former, and neo-liberalism is now consolidating its cultural hold, manufacturing a new type of person who is wholly bound (save for family) by the market and the media, and who can hence imagine no alternative. In that respect, major-party politics is over as anything other than a contest between rival plans to run nation-sized sections of the global market, and the people attracted to it will be those interested in implementing piecemeal programs, or in naked, amoral power. It's still worth having progressive-branded parties in power, and for people suited to that sort of politics to work within it. But it's the wrong place to look for transformative social movements. For people intent on the latter, one option is to try to make visible the profound contradictions between the current cultural and economic trajectories (which much of Hamilton's work does) – individually and globally – and both hasten and prepare for a time when those contradictions crack open and new possibilities emerge.

Guy Rundle

# WHAT'S LEFT?

Correspondence

## Andrew Norton

In a series of books since the mid-1990s, Clive Hamilton has attacked modern society as overly preoccupied with making and spending money. For the most part, political blame is apportioned to "neo-liberals" who, he alleges in *Affluenza* (2005), "have set out to promote higher consumption as the road to a better society". But the Left has also not escaped criticism, and in *What's Left? The Death of Social Democracy*, Hamilton elaborates on his view that social democrats share the neo-liberal assumption. They disagree over how actively governments should lessen inequalities of income and consumption, but not over whether rising income and consumption are desirable.

To Hamilton, this "compulsion to participate in consumer society" is no longer driven by material need but by "the belief of the great mass of people that to find happiness they must be richer, irrespective of how wealthy they already are". Yet Hamilton's work provides no direct evidence for this proposition. The evidence is circumstantial: inference from consumer behaviour and a Newspoll finding that nearly two-thirds of its respondents agreed with the statement that "You cannot afford to buy everything you really need." In a society that is very wealthy by comparison with the past and with elsewhere in the world, this figure is consistent with – though not proof of – an excessive preoccupation with money.

Yet other, similar research tells a different story. In the 2003 Australian Survey of Social Attitudes, for instance, only 20 per cent of those sampled indicated that they were finding it difficult to manage on their current household income. In the HILDA survey of the same year, reported on by Hamilton in a 2005 Australia Institute paper, around two-thirds of the people in this major longitudinal survey indicated satisfaction with their income. Satisfaction with standard of living, which incorporates the benefits of past purchases, was even higher than for income alone. The Australian Unity Wellbeing Survey consistently finds that around 77 per cent of its respondents are satisfied with their standard of living. Most people could find uses for more money than they earn. But preferring more money is not the same as believing that ever-greater amounts are needed for happiness.

Nor is the belief that money is the key to happiness evident in other survey research, which shows that Australians are willing to trade off more money to achieve other goals. In the 1999–2002 World Values Survey, Australians ranked sixteenth out of eighty nations in saying that leisure was "very important" in their lives. Fewer Australians than in most other countries thought good pay important in a job, while a greater number than in most other countries wanted jobs that were interesting, gave them an opportunity to achieve something and let them use their initiative. Australia Institute research corroborates the conclusion that material consumption is not all-important. When asked what would improve their quality of life, 75 per cent of those surveyed said more time with their family, and only 38 per cent opted for more money to buy things. The Institute's survey on "downshifting" (taking a lower income to pursue other life goals) found that nearly one-quarter of adults did this in the decade to 2002.

On this evidence, money is neither a source of majority discontent nor a goal to be pursued at the cost of all else. Commonsense was well ahead of the academic research in discovering that there is more to life than money. But if extra money is not essential to happiness, why do people prefer more of it? The simple and obvious answer is that if there is more to life than money, there is also more to life than happiness. Money can improve people's lives in many ways that won't necessarily feed into answers to questions like "All in all, how happy are you with your life these days?"

To some extent, as Hamilton argues in his *Quarterly Essay*, consumption choices help to define who we are: what we wear, the car we drive, the food we eat, the books we read, the films we see – all of these things send signals to others about the kind of person we are. Typically, Hamilton offers a reductive reading of this consumption activity. "We no longer want to keep up with the Joneses," he tells us, "we want to trump the Joneses by differentiating ourselves from them." But surely these signals are as much about associating as differentiating. Most people want to fit in more than stand out, and they do so partly through shared tastes in consumer goods and services. In the language of social democrats, people feel "socially excluded" if they cannot afford the purchases expected of members of their preferred social group.

Aside from their social uses, consumer goods and services offer private benefits that are unlikely to influence overall judgments of happiness but are real nonetheless. It's convenient to be able to read newspapers online, to microwave a meal quickly, or to make a call on a mobile while away from home. It's unlikely that the millions of Australians who purchased these electronic innovations expected to be happier as a result, but they did believe that they would be better off in more modest ways. Few people seem to be downshifting from these technological advances. Even the Australia Institute has a website, and its press releases offer Clive Hamilton's mobile number.

Hamilton won't accept that greater material wealth, except in the case of the very poor, can have positive effects. On the contrary, he asserts that the richest people in the world, the Americans, "are saying they are miserable" and that "it is the process of getting rich that causes the problems." And in his ten theses on consumption he maintains that "in rich countries increased consumption is now associated with declining wellbeing."

In a minority of cases, where people have muddled their priorities, this may be true. But as a generalisation it is not correct. While happiness has not increased as levels of consumption have gone up, nor has it decreased. It is remarkably stable. In the US, an overwhelming majority, more than 80 per cent, say that they are happy. This was as true in the latest survey, taken in 2005, as it was in the first, taken in 1946. Happiness questions are asked less frequently in Australia than in the US, but here, too, only a small minority regard themselves as unhappy. In the latest publicly available Australian survey, conducted in 2003, just 6.5 per cent of respondents rated themselves below the mid-point on a 0–10 happiness scale.

The "rash of psychological disorders – anxiety, depression, substance abuse" that Hamilton attributes to the consumer culture is hard to see in the wellbeing data. A 1995 happiness survey, like the 2003 poll, put the proportion of unhappy people at 6 per cent. Yet the Australian Bureau of Statistics' National Health Survey shows an increase in "mental and behavioural problems" from 5.9 per cent of the population in 1995 to 10.7 per cent in 2004–05. While some level of mental distress, as registered in the empirical research, is consistent with overall wellbeing, anxiety about one thing need not wipe out happiness felt about other things – these discrepant results require further investigation.

The increase in reported depression may not represent any real change in mental wellbeing. It could instead be the result of increased reporting or reclassifying other states of mind. Initiatives like *beyondblue* have reduced the stigma attached to mental illness, and presumably encouraged more people to acknowledge that they have a problem. New drugs are probably part of the explanation, too, providing a relatively easy chemical fix for those who are feeling down, but one that requires them to visit a doctor and say that they are depressed.

Even if more people have mental-health problems, is the "consumer culture" to blame? Consuming more is not, in itself, typically bad for wellbeing. In every survey, those who do the most consuming – those on higher incomes or with greater wealth – have higher average wellbeing than the poor or relatively poor. In the National Health Survey, people in the lowest income quintile are more than twice as likely as people in the highest income quintile to report mental-health issues. The employed, exposed to the market economy through their labour as well as their consumption, are less than half as likely as the unemployed to experience a mental-health problem.

These findings are more consistent with the social-democratic view than Hamilton's: a lack of resources is a risk factor for low wellbeing and poor mental health. And indeed, the Australian Survey of Social Attitudes found that 18 per cent of those saying they had difficulty managing on their current household income were unhappy, compared to 5 per cent of those who said that they were "coping" and 2 per cent of those who described themselves as "living comfortably" (though the vast majority of people with low incomes do not report unhappiness or mental-health problems).

Of particular concern in any analysis of wellbeing are the unemployed. As noted, the unemployed experience higher rates of reported mental-health problems than the employed. European research suggests that this is not just the result of lower income. Even in countries where unemployment benefits make up 70 or 80 per cent of an unemployed person's previous income, they still report significantly reduced wellbeing. German longitudinal research suggests that repeated unemployment has a "scarring" effect – even after work is found again, wellbeing is still below what it was before the initial job loss. Yet Hamilton's low-growth strategy can only increase the number of unemployed people. Only two years of negative or low growth in the early 1990s nearly doubled the unemployment rate, and we did not get back to pre-recession unemployment levels until 2004. Is it any wonder that social-democratic parties prefer economic growth to Hamilton's misery-creating policies?

Australian politics tends to operate through tackling perceived problems rather than implementing over-arching agendas such as Hamilton's "politics of wellbeing". But implicit in our recognition of problems is a rough conception of wellbeing that accords with the research on happiness and life satisfaction. Unemployment, low income and slow economic growth all make it harder to achieve the materially based aspects of wellbeing. Social-democratic parties – and, for that matter, all mainstream parties – sensibly focus on policies that aim to create the conditions for wellbeing. After that, it is up to individuals to make the right trade-offs between the competing components of a happy life.

Andrew Norton

# WHAT'S LEFT?

## Correspondence

### Ben Oquist

While Clive Hamilton provides an inspiring critique of what is wrong with much of contemporary Australian progressive politics, he does not match it with realistic and practical solutions to the malaise. Whatever one thinks of the Australian Greens, to write a 25,000-word *Quarterly Essay* on Australian politics from a progressive perspective and confine discussion of the Greens to three short paragraphs is shallow.

Hamilton suggests that it is only the evangelical churches that are providing "affirmation and value in part of being a community". Yet for me – and I believe thousands of other Australians – the Greens have provided meaning, purpose and direction that goes beyond self-interest, in a world that seems to have tilted too far towards individualism, materialism and consumerism.

Since the Australian Greens came together as a national force over ten years ago, the party has increasingly become the voice of progressive values and hope in Australian politics. Indeed, there is now a generation of Australians who have put their faith in the Greens – whether in response to Bob Brown's work in the Senate for West Papua and his action on climate change, or to the Greens' work in local and state government.

Despite his thoughtful analysis of progressive politics, the weakest point in Hamilton's essay is his conclusion that "all of this points to the need for a new political party." The Greens' vote has been steadily growing over the last decade and there is no sign of that trend wavering. The recent Tasmanian election saw the Greens retain their four seats, with more than one in six Tasmanians voting Green; and on the same day in South Australia, the Greens won a seat for the first time.

Hamilton's analysis is far too cursory. First, his charge that the Greens' emphasis on environmentalism limits the party's appeal is outdated. Mandatory sentencing, the *Tampa*, the Iraq war and West Papua – to name but a few – have put paid to that argument. Indeed, more-recent debate (hinted at by Hamilton) has focused on whether the party is environmental enough! While the challenge remains to present a coherent and credible economic policy free of the old dogmas of the Left, the "single-issue" tag is clearly fading.

Secondly, Hamilton's claim that the eventual departure of Bob Brown will test the enduring appeal of the party – while obviously true – fails to acknowledge the growing experience and skill of new Greens operating in state and federal parliament, not to mention the international success of the party. Seasoned operators such as Christine Milne, who led the Greens through the Tasmanian Labor–Green Accord, will no doubt rise to the challenge.

Hamilton's third argument – that Greens activists are ideologically wedded to fringe politics and work against broadening the party's appeal – is actually the challenge for the future: how to move from a protest, activist-based movement to a real power party. Even though the Greens have, in recent years, ruled in an alliance with both Labor and Liberal governments in Tasmania, it is partly true the party has so far failed to articulate how such experience could be transferred to a national level. This is curious, because unlike the Democrats or One Nation, the Greens have been in power at state and local level, holding positions of executive control in inner-city Melbourne, Byron Bay, and inner-city and eastern Sydney.

The Greens' great challenge remains: to convince Australia that they will deal effectively with real national power and deliver real progress towards a humanitarian and environmental society.

Why start another political party when there is a healthy and viable movement in place already? The Greens have a progressive ideology that is still developing and able to transcend the old dichotomy of Left and Right. With almost 10,000 members, an estimated 30,000 supporters and a million voters, the Greens possess a developing democratic base that, while still needing to represent its core supporters, is also finding new ways of connecting to the public.

The Greens have experience in government (with more than eighty local councillors and fifteen state and federal MPs) and a global network that could help deliver global solutions as the power of transnational corporations increasingly transcends domestic politics. This kind of established infrastructure takes years to develop.

Meanwhile, there are immediate, urgent challenges. The battle for all those engaged in practical progressive politics today should surely be to rescue the Senate from John Howard and Family First. This is not some pie-in-the-sky "we need a new political party" dream, but an urgent and practical project: the result may shape Australian politics for a generation to come.

Imagine a Senate after the next election where the Greens and Labor together had the numbers. Then imagine John Howard and Family First with the balance for another six years, ten years or more. Ensuring a progressive Senate is the struggle at hand, and to ignore it and speak abstractly about the death of progressive politics is to condemn Australia to another decade of conservatism.

No new party is going to be able to organise itself into a fully-fledged and effective political force in time to influence next year's poll. Any understanding of history or politics will tell you that political parties are not created overnight. They require blood, sweat and tears – just ask Bob Brown about the effort required to bring together disparate state and local Greens into a national force.

What the Greens need is constructive criticism from the likes of Clive Hamilton. Instead, on the evidence of *What's Left?*, he seems all too willing to dismiss the Greens in the shorthand style of conservative commentators such as Andrew Bolt, Christian Kerr and Piers Akerman.

Ben Oquist

# WHAT'S LEFT?

## Correspondence

### Don Aitkin

For some years now, a pervading theme in the great Australian conversation has been what the ALP has to do to get back into power. Not everybody engages in this conversation, of course. Many have different things on their mind. For some, the ALP is naturally out of power most of the time, and that is a good thing. For others, the ALP is part of our past, but not of our present and not at all of our future. There are those of advanced years who can remember when the ALP was world champion at shooting itself in the foot and was out of power for more than a quarter of a century. Nonetheless, it is our opposition and the alternative government, and its daily life is always interesting, indeed perhaps more interesting when it is in opposition than when it is in government.

Clive Hamilton's essay cuts deeper than many recent appreciations of Labor's predicament, and his conclusion that Labor is missing the plot by imitating the government and moving (if anything) to its right is persuasive. He summarises well a decade or more of research that shows that making us all wealthier doesn't make us correspondingly happier. I would agree that too many people have been caught up in an unending and unsuccessful attempt to buy happiness by working harder, earning more and "moving up". In the 1970s, when I was fond of sailing, I met people who thought that true happiness would lie in a larger boat than the one they already had. That didn't work either. But I'm not sure that Australians are "alienated", a term I grew to distrust after Marcuse took it up, because it seemed to provide a glib explanation for almost anything. Yet there seems to me little doubt that, in the broad, very many Australians who are more or less comfortably off, reasonably well educated, more or less happily married or partnered and in no real fear of a sudden end to it all, are nonetheless puzzled by the emptiness or pointlessness of life. As the young woman said after her first encounter with sex, "Is that all there is?" I had something of the same feeling after reading Hamilton's essay.

At its end, Hamilton offers ten theses on consumption, which conclude with the need to lower consumption ambitions and obtain "authentic identity". "A society built on core human values", he thinks, is the desire of most Australians, and he suggests that we need a "new politics of well-being". Then follow a number of policies that he thinks could form the basis of a party platform. The first two are about work, the next two about education and early childhood, the fifth about responsible advertising for children, the sixth is about the environment and the last is an appeal to have a better measure than GDP. I don't really disagree with any of them, but I don't think the ALP will find them an attractive platform for its electoral take-off, and they certainly wouldn't turn on those Australians who are looking for something more in life, let alone anyone who is genuinely alienated (which I take to mean feeling estranged from his or her society).

Why don't Hamilton's policies serve the purpose he intends? Because they don't deal with the central question: how do we formulate a meaningful life in this wealthy, autonomous, individualistic, materialistic, secular world? Clive Hamilton has certainly demolished the view that you can build a life around the pursuit of wealth itself, and the consumption that follows. The lotto ad that tells you that if you win "you can spend the rest of your life!" is perhaps too easy a target, but unquestionably television bombards us with the view that you can, and indeed should, build a life from working hard, earning a lot and consuming madly. Religion used to provide both the purpose for life and a text to follow in order to live life well, but our society has been abandoning religion steadily for the last two centuries, and quite rapidly in the last half-century. If we are to reduce the demands of work in our search for authentic human values, how are we to fill our time?

I think there is an answer, and it goes like this. Our experience of the last fifty years, along with a lot of research that points in the same direction, suggests that all human beings are born with high intelligence and creative potential. The growth of the university cohort and of the numbers involved in painting, music, theatre, sculpture and the other arts and crafts; the growth in the number of sports and the numbers seeking to be proficient in them – these trends offer a way forward. Look after the apparent "failures" of the educational system: it's better to persevere with them early than to have to lock them up later. Provide education in everything for everyone; extend people's capacities and talents. Ensure that we all have a number of outlets for our creativity. People who have begun to develop their creative capacities get a healthy burst of self-esteem and self-confidence, and are interested in extending their social networks to meet others with same interests. They are much less likely to be "alienated" than those who don't do so. They are rarely to be found in prison.

Part of the process involves educating young people that their basic task in life is to shape a person of whom they can be decently proud; that is, of course, themselves. Combining that with some education in self, sexuality and parenting would also be a good step forward. Do your best to ensure that people recognise that it's not enough just to consume; we also need to feel good about what we produce. And that applies politically: we can't leave everything to the politicians. A well-educated, creative, responsible and self-sufficient person ought to be a good citizen as well, unafraid to speak up for his or her values and to ensure that politicians are actually listening to their constituents.

Some such view of the world seems to me to be essential if we are to go along the path that Clive Hamilton maps out for us. And a lot of policies begin to have point and bite if you start with such a package. What sort of foreign policy should we have? How large should the Australian population be and what follows from that? Where do we start with a policy for the fragile Australian environment? How diverse a society can we afford? Policy domains like these require a good starting point and, with the greatest respect, I don't think that Clive Hamilton's analysis provides it. Wouldn't what I am suggesting cost a lot of money? Not all that much, and the outcomes should reduce the amount we spend on criminal justice and bandaid social welfare. We might even come out on top, financially. We are certainly wealthy enough as a society to embark on it.

Human beings cannot design and construct perfect societies, but we can always build better ones, and we ought to be doing so here. Yes, too many Australians are caught up in an ultimately empty life strategy, one that irritates them even when they appear to be successful. But to turn that around, reforming political parties have to have a vision of the better alternative, not simply recognise that their tactics are wrong. Until the ALP (or some other, as yet unknown political movement) grasps that truth, nothing very much is likely to change until external circumstances bring us once again to some kind of economic crisis.

And such an event will, given Australia's experiences in the depressions of the 1890s and 1930s, simply postpone the task once again.

Don Aitkin

# WHAT'S LEFT?

*Correspondence*

## Christopher Theunissen

Clive Hamilton's analysis suffers from being an exclusively economic and sociopolitical one. He identifies the issue of alienation as central, but neglects the psychological aspects of the problem that he identifies. This is more than an intellectual matter: it goes to the heart of how the issue of alienation in society might be comprehensively addressed.

Hamilton understands alienation solely at the level of political and social action. This is understandable given his intellectual background, but alienation also occurs within the context of the self. Disturbingly, matters of selfhood are rarely considered in formal political discourse. The self is seen as a private matter, and "private" is taken to mean that it is nobody's business except that of the individual in question. By implication, then, there are no public-interest issues in matters of selfhood. Yet this is absurd: by confining matters of the self (including the experience of alienation) to the domain of the private, the lack of a public-political discourse on matters of the self is justified and legitimised.

We are not merely consumers, nor are we only citizens or individuals struggling to survive economically. We are, first and foremost, human beings seeking meaning, purpose and identity – a point made forcefully by Hamilton. It follows, then, that alienation and selfhood need to be included in public debate – in much the same way that "mental health" is now becoming a legitimate matter for political consideration. Their inclusion will, of course, open up a potentially controversial and dangerous discourse, one in which citizens consider what is central to the purpose and meaning of their lives.

The issue of alienation becomes even more important when one of the goals that Hamilton sets for the citizenry is examined. Hamilton repeatedly emphasises the importance of happiness as a goal for the citizen in a social-democratic, post-industrial society. Yet joy is not a palliative to alienation. It is the psychological equivalent of administering paracetamol for a toothache: it provides at best temporary relief, but does not address the underlying source of pain and suffering. To paraphrase Martha Nussbaum, Hamilton should really have asked the question "How should a human being live?" rather than "What ought we do to increase happiness?" Happiness has its place, but living a purposive life offers greater potential for attaining true satisfaction, living a more complete life and protecting oneself against the threat of alienation.

Perhaps the most significant deficiency in Hamilton's essay is the absence of any coherent understanding of the psychological motives that underpin the drive toward "mindless" consumerism. While Hamilton acknowledges the role of anxiety in fostering conservatism, he appears not to appreciate the role of envy in driving a competitive dynamic between citizens. It is this combination of anxiety and status envy that is most likely responsible for the dual phenomena of the retreat from the social and the unempathic competitiveness that seem to be hallmarks of our society. Seen in this light, the mindless accumulation of inanimate objects is an understandable (if undesirable) "solution" to the malaise of alienation. Unfortunately, Hamilton's analysis pays scant attention to this issue, nor does it prescribe any systematic response to the psychological dilemmas involved. The potential solutions he offers in his conclusion appear to be little more than axiomatic principles, which rely in part upon institutions such as the employer class, the advertising industry and neo-liberal ideologues undoing the very things they have sought to implement for the past three decades. These, of course, are the sectors of the community that have most effectively exploited angst and envy to serve their own narrow interests.

Of all of the prescriptions offered by Hamilton, the most psychologically salient and important one is that of investing in early childhood. Curiously, this prescription is given the most cursory treatment of any of Hamilton's recommendations, yet it is clear from decades of psychological research that it is probably the most significant factor in the development of coherent selfhood (and therefore protection against alienation). Hamilton's analysis is here typical of economic structuralists: get the conditions right and the rest will take care of itself. Herein lies the key flawed assumption in Hamilton's position. It assumes that if people are simply left to themselves with sufficient time (and we already know that they have the wealth), then alienation will be dispelled. Decades of clinical research and clinical experience tell us that this is not the case. The types of legislative and technocratic interventions prescribed by Hamilton will not address the salient psychological issues: a deeper understanding of the basis of envy, angst and alienation is required. Not only are social and political variables involved, but also a complex array of co-occurring psychological, attachment and relational factors that together produce the condition we refer to as "alienation".

Hamilton sees the solution, in part, as one of shared parental leave for the first two years of an infant's life. While this is laudable, the literature on development, attachment theory and child psychopathology tells us that identity and selfhood are complex processes. We need a wider, deeper debate on child-care, the family–work balance and the function of mothering and fathering in our culture. The evidence from these literatures might force us to consider directions that do not easily fit with our prevailing ideological assumptions.

Christopher Theunissen

# WHAT'S LEFT?

*Response to Correspondence*

Clive Hamilton

Rebecca Huntley and Guy Rundle have limped rather than leapt to the defence of social democracy and the ALP. Rundle endorses one of the moral presuppositions of my analysis: that a progressive party must address the needs of low-paid workers and welfare recipients (other than the middle-class kind), but politically it cannot make that the centrepiece of its appeal to the public. He seems to be saying that, for electoral reasons, it cannot; whereas I am saying that it *should* not. In ways I detail in the essay, modern consumer capitalism has changed the consciousness of a large portion of the population: these people no longer identify with the appeals to social justice of old, both because they are much more self-absorbed and because they have come to believe that misfortune is in large measure self-induced. This is the dark side of prosperity.

The fundamental political question for progressives is how to transform the consciousness of this prosperous middle two-thirds of the population. Some of my social-democratic critics (not represented here) have made appeals to the enduring egalitarianism of Australians (although at other times the same critics bemoan the spread of individualism and selfishness). Yet it must be conceded that the egalitarian spirit we cleave to has entered the realm of myth, where it is craftily exploited by Prime Minister Howard. Those who are genuinely doing it tough will be waiting a long time if they must rely on electoral expression of the egalitarian spirit.

Instead of appealing to some residual sense of social justice, the approach of the politics of wellbeing involves posing some very personal questions to the prosperous middle. Now that you are well-off, are you happy? What does your life amount to? What are the personal costs of your materialistic desires? What would truly make your life more worthwhile and fulfilling? Rundle seems to think it futile to pose these questions, for while the populace often feels anxious, empty and depressed, they have become habituated to such feelings and indeed are "deeply at home in a consumer culture". The market has created a new human, he asserts, one so bound by the ideology of the market that he or she can imagine no alternative.

In truth, there is a mass of evidence pointing the other way; Australians are deeply ambivalent about the consumer life and yearn for something more fulfilling. The pointlessness of the consumer life is a deeply felt sentiment, one that requires ever-greater personal effort to suppress, and ever-more spending and creativity by the marketers to disguise. The downshifters I refer to in the essay, representing perhaps a fifth of the population, are a sign of the limits to these efforts. In her contribution, Huntley provides some more evidence of this deep ambivalence, acquired from her study of Generation Y.

In suggesting that I want to persuade people of the "joys of austerity", Rundle repeats a common misrepresentation of my argument. This is in keeping with those, like Andrew Norton, who claim that my argument is "anti-growth", that I am saying recession is to be preferred, that I am against consuming, and that I believe money is evil. In fact, I am not opposed to economic growth, nor to high incomes or engaging in consumption. What I argue against is the *attachment* to these things, the extraordinary power we invest in growth and consumption to make the world go round and to rescue us from meaningless lives. The life of the ascetic may be just as much governed by money as that of the most materialistic aspirational. If a religious metaphor helps, my position has more in common with the detachment of Buddhism than the denial of Calvinism. I repudiate the hair-shirt as much as the Calvin Klein one, for the attachment to the garment may be equally unhealthy.

I have tried to make plain my position here so often that the failure of my critics to understand it stands as a testament to the grip of black-and-white thinking, i.e. if you oppose my position, then you must support its negation. It is a means of defining the world in terms of one's own position and excluding a new understanding.

## Social-democratic defeatism

The overwhelming sense I get from the contributions of Rundle and Huntley is that of resignation. An air of desperation, or at least despondency, pervades their claims that the ALP can renew itself. While they are to be admired for their perseverance, their argument would be more persuasive if they were to indicate from where this renewal might spring. Is it fermenting away in Young Labor? Are the branches becoming bolshie? Where are the ginger groups and think-tanks? Where is the tumult of ideas? As Huntley notes, Latham's ascendancy offered a taste of it, but the party, stung by the outcome of its experiment, has retreated to the bunkers. We search in vain for a hook on which to hang a shred of optimism.

Worryingly, Rundle's gamble for renewal hinges on the possibility that the self-satisfied prosperous middle will be brought to its knees by an economic collapse, perhaps triggered by untoward events in the Chinese or US economies. Labor could then ride triumphant into Canberra on the ruins of the economy, and on this basis "progressive elements in the party would be revived." Rundle dreams of returning to a world of deprivation where social-democratic ideals would once more be relevant. What a miserable view of the future. It is indeed possible that Labor could win by default under such circumstances; but it would not deserve to win. And it is mere wishful thinking to argue that progressive elements would be revived. They were not when Hawke and Keating came to power on the back of a recession; precisely the opposite happened. The Left buckled and stood by as, in caucus and in cabinet, it suffered one defeat after another. In such circumstances, it would not be the Left of the party that surged ahead but the Right, the guardians of "sound economic management".

The defeatism and deprivation-nostalgia of many social democrats – Rundle declares that Tony Blair's Labour Party is as good as it gets! – reflects a failure of imagination rooted in a sort of post-modern nihilism. Had the first social democrats, or the founders of feminism, been so pessimistic about the possibilities of social change, a century of social progress would have been lost. Personally, I draw more inspiration from the neo-liberals. Although their worldview is repugnant to me, in the 1970s and 1980s their radicalism and fervour inspired a political movement that transformed the world. And, for all his shortcomings, Mark Latham exhibited the most vital characteristic of a modern progressive leader: a burning belief that, despite all of the obstacles, social change is possible.

The emotional capitulation of the Left of the Labor Party has robbed it of any chance of effecting social change. But perhaps I am being too harsh; let me instead pose a very simple test that, if passed, would cause me to recant, or at least reconsider, my jaundiced view. Let the Left of the party in the New South Wales Parliament cross the floor and vote against the privatisation of the Snowy Hydro scheme. It's a simple test of commitment to social-democratic principles.

## Are we unhappy?

Andrew Norton of the Centre for Independent Studies, a neo-liberal think-tank, understandably devotes his response to examining, and rejecting, the single factual assumption on which my entire case rests: that rapid increases in money incomes in industrialised countries have not made the citizenry feel any better off. For if people are no happier now than they were, say, thirty years ago, what was the point of two decades of "reform", which was justified by one argument above all: that freeing and extending markets would liberate productive capacity, thereby making us richer and better off?

It is not possible here to reply in detail by debating the wealth of evidence bearing on this question, so let me make just six points.

Norton concedes that the evidence does not show an increase in reported happiness over the decades. This is in itself a massive concession, given the unceasing promises of a better life that the advocates of neo-liberalism in the think-tanks, corporations, parliaments and newspapers have been making for decades.

Having conceded that extra money does not lead to greater happiness, Norton next abandons the foundational premise of neoclassical economics – the utility function – by suggesting that there is "more to life than happiness". Surprisingly, he deviates from the neo-liberal script by referring not to the priority of freedom over happiness, but to other reasons for accumulating more money. These include what he calls social acceptance, convenience and "being better off in more modest ways". How these cannot be aspects of overall happiness or life satisfaction is beyond my ken.

Although at times I have used them myself, measures of "happiness" based on surveys that assess self-reported life satisfaction have little meaning, and Norton's use of them cuts no ice. The usual measure of happiness, self-reported life satisfaction, is usually gauged simply by asking people by phone or in person if they are happy with their lives. For a number of reasons, in this situation most people will say they are happy or, more accurately, not admit that they are unhappy. The method conceals more than it reveals. This is a big and complex question that I do not have space to explore, but let me illustrate my point with an anecdote. I recently met a man who told me that he works with the Catholic Church. Sometimes he goes on camping retreats with groups of parishioners, typically aspirational voters with McMansions and all of the trappings of material success. If asked if they were happy, they would undoubtedly declare that they are; after all, with all of the trappings, why wouldn't they be? Yet, my friend told me, when sitting around the camp fire after a couple of glasses of red, it does not take long before they begin to talk tearily of the pointlessness of their lives and their yearning to do something more meaningful.

A comprehensive measure of psychological health would be the best measure of the state of the nation's wellbeing. Longitudinal data are patchy, but there is a consensus among experts that our mental health has been in long-term decline. The same applies in the US and Britain.

One can agree with Norton that consuming more "is not in itself typically bad". On the other hand, a good argument can be made that above a certain threshold, consuming more of many things is bad, including too much food, alcohol, gambling and television viewing. And I think most would agree that, for more subtle reasons, Imelda Marcos had too many shoes. Yet my argument, made at length in my previous books, is that it is not consumption itself, but the *culture of consumption* — our obsessive materialism, and the way the values of the market invade everyday life — that is pernicious. There is now a mass of evidence — some of it presented in Tim Kasser's excellent book *The High Price of Materialism* — showing that those who are more materialistic in their life-orientation are less happy, more psychologically troubled and have more corrosive personal relationships. Yet our political and economic systems encourage and validate precisely this sort of materialistic behaviour and life-orientation.

I won't respond to Norton's suggestion that my "low-growth strategy" can only increase unemployment and is therefore "misery-creating". Norton knows from reading my other works that I have dealt with this objection at length, so his argument here is just a debating trick.

While Norton's response is, on the face of it, a defence of neo-liberalism, I think he and his fellow neo-liberals secretly hope to defend the ALP from this new line of criticism, because if the ALP remains as it is currently constituted, its election would represent no real threat to the great advances of neo-liberalism of the last two decades.

## The Greens

Some members of the Greens have been disappointed at my apparent dismissal of the party as a viable major progressive force. My argument in the essay, which perhaps reflected the victory of the head over the heart, was not meant to belittle the sterling efforts of hundreds, even thousands, of committed Greens supporters. They have done well to garner up to 10 per cent of the vote over the last decade, although it must be worrying that much of this voter support appears soft and prone to drift back to the major parties. The real test is whether the Greens can win over, and secure, the next 10 per cent of the vote, and then the 10 per cent after that. I cannot see that happening.

Ben Oquist reminds us that the Greens have become the clarion voice on a number of progressive issues abandoned by Labor, notably ones associated with human rights. Like many progressives, I am thankful that they have filled this gap. But in making the transition from single-issue to multi-issue party, the Greens have moved beyond a coherent environmental philosophy to a position that has no apparent philosophical underpinning other than liberal humanism.

It is true that the Greens have broadened their appeal and are now as much the party of human rights and social justice as of the environment. But can the Greens replace the ALP by being the party of Left causes? Can it win the support of a large portion of the Australian populace by taking up the issues on which Labor has gone soft? I argue in the essay that the transformation of the psyche of the broad middle classes under two or more decades of neo-liberalism and the culture of consumption has weakened Australians' commitment to human rights and their compassion for the underprivileged.

Some time ago I came to accept that there is a distinct limit to the appeal of environmentalism in a world defined by consumerism. No matter how dire the threat of environmental catastrophe, I believe that so long as people define themselves in large measure by their consumption spending and their lifestyle, they would sooner die than radically change their behaviour. In a sense, environmentalism is asking people to kill themselves and then find a new identity. Instead of sending the message that we are doomed unless we all change our ways, it will prove far more effective as a political strategy to ask people whether their high consumption and wasteful lifestyles actually make them happy. Confirming overseas research, our work at the Australia Institute shows that when this question is posed, most people say "no".

## Policy proposals

The essay concludes with a number of proposals for policies that could be adopted by a new party committed to the politics of wellbeing. They were included to circumvent the criticism that I have no positive alternative to put forward. Some have criticised me for being anodyne, with proposals that could easily be adopted by Labor. I am sympathetic to the critics (such as Don Aitkin) who say that I do not go nearly far enough. But in a sense these criticisms miss the mark. The politics of wellbeing I propose calls for a radical new social vision, one that relegates the market and consumption behaviour to a much-restricted place – through legislation where necessary – and envisages a democratic politics that facilitates and encourages what might be called authentic ways of living. One might draw an analogy with the women's movement, which called for a few legislative changes to eliminate formal discrimination, but was in truth committed to a far-reaching transformation of the consciousness of women and men and the way in which they relate to each other.

*Alienation*

Don Aitkin and Christopher Theunissen go straight to the core of my argument, which concerns the nature of alienation; they suggest that I do not go far enough in practice (Aitkin) or analytically (Theunissen). Perhaps I underestimated my readers' capacity to be challenged, for in fact not only do I accept the broad thrust of their critiques, but I believe that they themselves have not gone far enough.

Aitkin takes up my argument that the central problem of modern consumer society is that of alienation, and that a new progressive politics should be built on a recognition of this instead of outdated notions of deprivation. While averse to the term "alienation", he accepts the proposition that Australians, immersed in their affluence, are beset by doubts about consumer life. He says that the policies I put forward as the basis for a new politics of wellbeing fall short of the mark, and argues instead that the most promising approach involves transforming our system of education to ensure that everyone – and he means everyone – has their capacities, talents and creativity extended as far as they can be.

This is close to the "capabilities" approach of Amartya Sen and Martha Nussbaum and it is a policy proposal that I would endorse strongly; in fact, it is prominent in the Manifesto for Wellbeing I have developed with others (see <www.wellbeingmanifesto.net>). Yet, as a means of social transformation and as the basis for a new progressive politics, it falls well short. The capabilities approach is a useful halfway house on the road to providing a fulfilling life for all. It is infinitely preferable to the pursuit of "happiness", interpreted as short-term gratification, which more often than not serves as a means of covering up the loss of meaning. Alienation runs deeper than Aitkin suggests, but it really would have been stretching the patience of readers of the essay for me to expatiate on that subject. I thus reverted, perhaps mistakenly, to shorthand, arguing that we can aim for a "happier" society.

In a striking contribution, Theunissen goes much more directly to the notion of alienation and berates me for confining the analysis of the essay exclusively to the economic and socio-political. He argues persuasively that the usual distinction used by critics of neo-liberalism between citizens and consumers is inadequate because it fails to account for our nature as humans seeking meaning. On this basis he urges us to pursue a philosophy of eudaimonism as the answer to modern alienation, which he defines (more helpfully than Aitkin) as a loss of connection with both self and other. In fact, in *Growth Fetish* I make precisely this argument for going beyond superficial and ultimately unfulfilling notions of happiness, and describe a political philosophy that I call eudemonism. Building on Aristotle's work (which is not without its ambiguities), I argue for an organisation of society that promotes the full realisation of human potential through, in the first instance, proper appreciation of the sources of wellbeing.

Theunissen criticises my essay for failing to acknowledge the problem of the self by implicitly consigning it to a private realm beyond politics and social analysis. Yet a substantial part of the essay is devoted to individualisation and the problem this poses for the construction of identity. The new politics I propose is rooted in this very transformation of the nature of the individual and the struggle for self-definition, one that renders social democracy anachronistic. It is too much to ask of a political essay that it expand on the subject of the self and its variations. But that lack of detail ought not to obscure the differences between the three fundamentally divergent conceptions of the individual – and the self that dwells in it – that underlie social democracy, neo-liberalism and the politics of wellbeing.

Theunissen, too, is pushing me further than I thought prudent to go in the essay, but it is in a direction that meets little resistance from me. In response to his criticism that I pay scant attention to the motivations for mindless accumulation of inanimate objects, I would ask only that he refer to *Growth Fetish* and *Affluenza*, where this topic is discussed at length.

Like the other contributors, Theunissen finds my policy proposals an irresistible target, arguing that they are an inadequate response to complex psychological problems; that they are essentially technocratic and "operate only at a political and social level". This is really too much! Theunissen has forgotten that we are operating in the political and social realms, not the psychologist's consulting room. The weakness of his contribution is that, while willing to point to a series of failures and lapses on my part, he shies away from any alternative policy or political direction.

## Political strategy

Let me finish with some observations on what I suspect is the most fundamental but barely visible difference between me and many of my critics. It has its basis in the understanding of history. In formulating a political strategy, anyone who argues for radical social change must start from where we are and yet not be trapped by the present. The policy proposals I put forward in the essay are in the service of the former, yet the social analysis avoids the latter. In order to escape the clutches of the present, one must identify the seeds of change within the prevailing dispensation. At the broadest level, I believe that these are to be found in the profound uneasiness that arises from the contradiction between the promises of affluence and the fundamental human desire to live a worthwhile life. While at the superficial level most Australians say that they would like to have more money and material things (indeed, that they "need" them), and mostly behave accordingly, one does not have to delve far beneath the surface to discover that Australians have very little faith that affluence can give them what they truly want.

Those who can see no further than the superficial expressions of desire are inescapably trapped in the present and can do no other than tinker at the edges. For such people, who number among them dispirited social democrats, change cannot be organic but can only be thrust upon us from without, by way of economic collapse or environmental catastrophe. In that case, the only sensible course of action is to sit back and wait for external events to occur.

It is a long time since progressives were at the forefront of social change; most have expended their energy resisting the radicalism of the neo-liberals and protecting past gains. Laudable though these efforts were, progressives have found themselves to be conservatives by default. It is therefore to the freshness of younger generations, to the Gen Yers and younger Gen Xers, that we must look to find the champions of the new politics of wellbeing.

Clive Hamilton

**Don Aitkin** was Vice-Chancellor and President of the University of Canberra from 1991 to 2002. His *Stability and Change in Australian Politics* was first published in 1977. *What Was It All For? The Reshaping of Australian Society after 1950* was published last year, and he is currently working on a sequel, *Creative Australia: A Confident Vision for our Country*.

**Clive Hamilton**'s book *Growth Fetish* was published in 2003, and his most recent book is *Affluenza*, co-authored with Richard Denniss. Hamilton is executive director of the Australia Institute, an independent think-tank based at the Australian National University.

**Rebecca Huntley** has worked as an academic and political staffer and is now a freelance writer. She is the author of *The World According to Y: inside the new adult generation*. She is a member of the ALP.

**Amanda Lohrey** began her working life as a lecturer in political science at the University of Tasmania. She has since published many articles on Australian political life, including Quarterly Essay 8, *Groundswell: The Rise of the Greens*, and two political novels, *The Morality of Gentlemen* and *The Reading Group*. More recently her novels include *The Philosopher's Doll* and the award-winning *Camille's Bread*.

**Andrew Norton** is a Research Fellow at the Centre for Independent Studies and also edits its magazine, *Policy*. He co-edited *A Defence of Economic Rationalism* and is the author of *The Unchained University* and a regular contributor to newspapers on higher education issues.

**Ben Oquist** helped establish the Australian Greens and was an adviser to Bob Brown for ten years in Canberra. He currently works on the campaign for self-determination for West Papua.

**Guy Rundle** is the writer of political satires performed by Max Gillies and the author of Quarterly Essay 3, *The Opportunist: John Howard and the Triumph of Reaction*, published in 2001.

**Christopher Theunissen** is Senior Lecturer in the School of Psychology at Edith Cowan University.

www.ingramcontent.com/pod-product-compliance
Lightning Source LLC
LaVergne TN
LVHW061303060426
835510LV00014B/1850